TYING THE PERFECT KNOT

A Practical Guide To Beautiful Hindu Weddings

Padmakar Gangatirkar

The characters and events portrayed in this book are fictitious. Any similarity to real persons, living or dead, is coincidental and not intended by the author. However, the photos are from real weddings, shown with the written permission from their owners.

The author has interpreted some rituals based on his own views and the present demographics of the couples, primarily in the USA.

ISBN-13: 9798458248419

Cover design by: Mangal Gangatirkar
The cover picture depicts the essence of the Hindu Wedding Ceremony, the worship of the Sacred Fire, the Lord of the Home.

Library of Congress Control Number: 2018675309
Printed in the United States of America

1st Edition: October 2021
Vijayadashami (Dashahara)

CONTENTS

PREFACE

I became a Hindu priest out of necessity. There were very few priests in the nineteen eighties to serve the first generation Hindu community in America. I was "qualified" to be a priest, a Paṇḍita (पण्डित), as a born Brāhmaṇa (ब्राह्मण) and having studied the scriptural language and having done a few religious rituals back home in India in my formative years. With that limited background, my friends would ask me to perform various sacraments for them, for which I had to study our ancient scriptures and philosophies in depth. Being an engineer, I questioned every religious ritual for its meaning and thus I learned the logical, scientific and spiritual aspects of the Hindu philosophy. That study has continued to this date, enabling me to deliver deeper understanding of Hindu rituals for my clients.

Since the late 1990s, I have officiated many Indo-American

weddings in various parts of the USA, Mexico, Costa Rica and even India. I work with the parents and the couple before the wedding to understand their specific desires and traditions and then customize their ceremony. After the wedding, I analyze all my events critically for what worked well and what did not in order to continuously improve my contribution of the overall wedding experience.

The driving force behind this book are the many letters that I received from the attendees stating that the ceremonies were perfect, ideal, educational and the best they have witnessed. I wanted to share my approach with the future couples, their parents, other priests, wedding planners and those interested in Hindu culture so that all can benefit from that approach. In addition, I still find many people repeating the same missteps that result in less than perfect wedding experiences, for the hosts and the guests. I share those incidences with the readers so that they can try to avoid those situations.

There are many books, which give complete description and meaning of all Saṃskṛta (संस्कृत) mantras associated with the wedding ceremony. All priests are well versed in them. What this book offers is how to do them more effectively by connecting with audience, explaining the logic and significance behind them, in about an hour but still keeping their full sanctity.

This book is a practical guide how to perform the wedding and pre-wedding rituals from an officiant's perspective, taking into consideration the present demographics of the couples. It tells the story of a representative Indo-American wedding. The characters, events and locations in this book are realistic but fictional. Any resemblance to actual wedding and characters is purely coincidental. I provide various guidelines for a perfect wedding with pictures illustrating different environments, cultures and traditions.

It has been a privilege and an honor to officiate Hindu weddings of young Indo-American brides and grooms. I have met many wonderful people who have also become life long friends. I have learnt a lot about our own Hindu philosophy with its very deep and spiritual roots. Therefore, I am thankful to all who asked me to perform this important milestone in their lives and those who sent very complimentary remarks after their weddings.

I am thankful to my colleague and fellow paṇḍita, Mr. Anil Shelat who meticulously went through every chapter and made many valuable suggestions about the pre-wedding and wedding ceremonies. Dr. Dilip Amin and Mr. David Chapin provided insightful comments on the various aspects of Hindu weddings.

My friends Gopi Advani, Sue Wiley, Chary Tamirisa and Vashishtha Sharma reviewed the manuscript and contributed their own experiences. I also appreciate the constant encouragement of my brother-in-law, Bhau Dhavale, to write this book.

I am very thankful to Pramod Mehta, Pradip Mehta, Archna Tripathi, Anil Pande, Tarun Parikh and Vaishali Phansalkar who willingly sent the photos of the weddings of their sons and daughters and gave me permission to publish them in this book. These pictures accurately bring out the essence of the Hindu ceremonies; the meaningful rituals, their sanctity, the pageantry as well as the happiness that surrounds this once-in-a-life event. The pictures are from the weddings of Ashvini and Rajiv, Sonia and Matt, Pooja and Karan, Sonya and Geoff, Gargi and Amod, Anisha and Sunil,and Lauren and Shivanshu.

All paṇḍitas perform Hindu rituals in Saṃskṛta (संस्कृत) language. Saṃskṛta words are difficult to translate accurately or to spell them correctly in the English alphabet. I have written these words using the International Alphabet of Saṃskṛta Transliteration (IAST) and in the Devanagari Script. The appendix includes the glossary for key words.

Finally, I am greatly indebted to my wife, Mangal, and daughter, Seema for their continuous guidance and suggestions while writing this book.

Padmakar Gangatirkar

1. INTRODUCTION

The origin of the phrase "Tying the Knot" comes from the medieval era of Celtic weddings. The purpose of that hand fasting ceremony was to bind the couple together and make them one.

The Hindu Weddings have been binding the couple ever since the Vedic Times, even before the 15th century BC. They call it "Vadhu-Vara-Bandhanam (वधू वर बन्धनं)", binding the bride and the groom, physically, mentally and spiritually, in many different ways.

The Hindu wedding ceremony is the most continuously practiced ceremony in the world, deeply spiritual and very meaningful. Why do we still need to make it perfect? Well, here are some reasons.

The wedding is not an isolated incident in our Hindu lives. It is one-step of the Hindu Way of Life, with the previous sacraments before the wedding as its foundation. The primary objective of the marriage is not just love but continuity of the life cycle with progeny and carrying out the householder duties in the right and noble manner. With those objectives firmly established, the married householders become the bedrock of any community. We need to emphasize this very important aspect of the Hindu wedding.

Further, with more than 50% second generation Hindus marrying non-Hindus, we need to address the realities of the present demographics of Indo-American couples. This necessitates modifications to the ceremony without compromising the fundamentals of the Hindu philosophy while being sensitive towards American values. The wedding rituals need to be more meaningful, more logical and smooth flowing in the new environment.

Still, the whole ceremony needs to be an enjoyable event! After all, it is the happiest event of the couple's lives along with their parents!

Finally, we all have attended weddings in India as well as in the western countries. Barring few ceremonies, most of the attendees do not comprehend the full significance of these rituals. Many priests may not explain the deeper significance of the Saṃskṛta (संस्कृत) verses to them. The traditional ceremonies can be too long and even tedious, resulting in some socialization among guests for relief! Therefore, it may be helpful to improve the way they conduct the ceremony to maintain the sanctity, formality and serenity of this most important event in their client's lives.

Those are the primary reasons why I wrote this book. It will guide you on how to conduct an ideal ceremony, in about an hour, with full ritual content reflecting the present demographics, with focus on the goals of a married life, in a meaningful and logical manner, all delivered in an enjoyable way.

"Binding the Couple" by various means is a simple procedure but getting there may not be that easy due to many minor and major hurdles. If you are planning a Hindu wedding in any foreign country, you may have many questions about how to plan all the wedding events.

Here are some questions that the brides and groom ask me frequently.

- How can we have a short but beautiful Hindu wedding ceremony?
- Will you explain and communicate the significance of the rituals?
- Can we modify the ceremony to reflect our views and traditions?
- How do we resolve intercultural and interfaith issues?

The parents whose son or daughter is getting married want to know how to plan and conduct a Hindu wedding in the western atmosphere.

- How do we resolve conflicts between the parents and the couple?
- How do we make sure that our Hindu values do not get lost?
- How do we manage so many events efficiently?
- What is a good Muhurta (मुहूर्त) - auspicious time- for

the wedding?

- How do we find a suitable venue?

Some want to be a Hindu wedding priest for one or two weddings only. Some professional priests want to do the ceremony much more effectively to a western audience based on their client requests.

On the other hand, many are interested in general Hindu philosophy and want to know more about its wedding traditions. Alternatively, you may be attending a Hindu Wedding and curious about the rituals. Some wedding planners want to know more details about the various rituals so that they can manage thier event s better with all the logistics involved.

If you find yourself in any of these situations, well, this book will guide you in the right direction. It is a practical approach to reduce the anxieties of parents and the would-be-couple, a guide to Hindu priests and an introduction to a Hindu way of Life to all. If you are planning a wedding, this guide will make your planning easy and you will have a beautiful, enjoyable and successful wedding.

Many concerns of second-generation weddings in America do not arise for the weddings in India. Since almost all marriages are "arranged", the weddings happen with parental and family approvals. A high level of compatibility exists between the bride, the groom and their families in all key matters. Intergenerational differences exist but to a much lesser degree in Indian families where old age and old traditions are well respected. At the wedding itself, there are neither time constraints nor any formalities; it is mostly a social event for attendees.

In this book, I explain an approach for an ideal wedding based on best of both- a Hindu and a Christian ceremony- with an example of an Indo-American wedding in Houston, USA. This example does not address all the rituals, all the customs for all the wedding traditions in all the regions of India. However, the guidelines should be applicable to all Hindu weddings.

The story starts with an initial excitement of the engagement, then goes through various concerns, issues, compromises, resolutions, planning, and ends with a successful wedding. You may not experience these specific issues or may not do all these specific events. Nevertheless, this story will help answer your questions, help resolve your issues and reduce your worries and you will enjoy your wedding thoroughly.

In order to illustrate the various rituals, I have used pictures from different weddings! Therefore, you will see our representative couple, Neha and Ravi, in many different forms throughout the book.

Do the guidelines in this book result in a great wedding? In the Appendix, I have included letters from the parents and the couples who thought their wedding ceremonies were beautiful, enjoyable and memorable. These comments should help the priests understand what considerations are important to their clients.

Do things go wrong? Of course they do! The Appendix also describes many events that did not go as well as the couple, their parents and I had hoped. Almost all those incidents were avoidable with the guidelines given in this book. Nowadays, I do advise my clients if some of these situations may apply to their weddings and leave it up to them to revise their plans if possible.

This book is not about what to wear, what to give, how to plan Saṃgīta (संगीत) or reception or what are the various costs. It is also not about each wedding step with in-depth translation of each Saṃskṛta mantra. Instead, this is a practical, logical, a "how to" guide for planning and carrying out a modern Hindu wedding.

Enjoy the wedding!

2. IMAGINING THE WEDDING

It was an early March morning when I was busy writing the script for a wedding I was going to officiate the following Saturday, when the phone rang.

"Hello Paṇḍitaji! This is Kavita, from Houston. Do you remember me?"

The name sounded familiar but I could not remember the face.

"I helped you at Maya's wedding. That was almost four years back! And we were seated at the same table for the evening reception."

2.1 Initial Excitement

Yes, I clearly remembered Maya's wedding. I had officiated that Indian-Chinese-Scottish wedding in Dallas. It was at this wedding that I connected the Celtic "Tying the Knot" tradition to the Hindu wedding of binding the couple with various means, physically, mentally and spiritually.

At that wedding, Ryan was the Scottish groom, dressed in a Scottish kilt. Maya was the Hindu-Chinese bride, dressed in a long white gown with red ties, a tradition from her mother's side. Ryan's sister tied their garments together, the Hindu way, just before they circled the sacred fire.

Their picture really shows the all-inclusive nature of a Hindu ceremony, which binds the couple together, on their journey to a strong family, represented by the symbol of a prosperous home, the sacred fire.

We sat with Kavita and her husband, Vijay, at the same table during the evening reception. Vijay was a project manager in a multinational company and Kavita worked as a pharmacist; both in Houston. Over the dinner, we had discussed many considerations regarding the Hindu weddings in America. They had casually remarked that they would call me if their daughter ever decided to get married.

"Hello Kavita? How are you?" I asked.

"Our daughter, Neha, is getting married!" I heard a big excitement in her voice.

She further told me how Ravi, Neha's fiancé, had proposed to her on New Year's Eve in San Francisco soon after the fireworks burst over the Bay Bridge. Ravi had arranged a dinner cruise with all their close friends that evening. As soon as the New Year's greetings were over, he kneeled down and asked Neha whether she would marry him; to which she said yes and burst into tears.

Soon thereafter, Vijay had called Ravi's father, Ashok, to share each other's excitement about the upcoming wedding. He suggested that they all get together for an engagement party on Valentine's Day in Houston. Ashok, a family physician and his wife Susan, a registered nurse, were both working at a regional hospital in Burlington, Vermont. He and Susan were married in early nineteen-eighties, by traditional Hindu ceremony in India. They would be delighted to travel to Houston to escape the bitter Vermont cold for a few days. They were happy that Ravi had finally decided to marry Neha, whom they had met before and had liked her because of her caring nature and Indo-American upbringing.

Vijay told me about the engagement party, attended by Ravi's parents and their daughter, Asha. Neha's older brother, Neal, also had come from Dallas with his girlfriend, Lisa.

They had tossed many ideas about the wedding but had not yet decided on any of the options. There were significant differences of opinions about everything between the couple, the siblings and the parents.

It is very rare that the hosts contact me about my availability before the couple and the parents have even decided the date and the venue for the wedding! Kavita wanted to discuss the auspicious dates before deciding the venue. Neha and Ravi were wondering why that was so important.

This was just the beginning. Sensing some disagreements, I wanted to know where the parents and the couple were coming from; so I asked for a little more background.

Ravi was born and raised in Burlington, Vermont. With an Indian father and an American mother, he and his sister Asha grew up celebrating both cultures. Susan was very progressive and had taught them fundamentals of both the religions.

Ravi's favorite activity during his growth years was to hike Mt. Mansfield and Mt. Washington. After high school, he went to University of California at Berkeley for his undergraduate degree in Computer Science. Somehow, he did not want to follow the medical profession like his dad and mom; he left that family tradition to his younger sister, Asha.

Ravi had moved to San Jose after his graduation to work for a well-known IT company. An outdoor person, he had joined a local Hiking Club; a highly diverse group of professionals from different countries and ethnicities.

Neha was born and raised in Houston. She had moved to Austin to attend University of Texas for her law degree. After graduation, she too moved to San Jose to work for an intellectual-property-law company. At one of her friend's insistence, Neha joined the same hiking club of which Ravi was a member.

Vijay and Kavita were naturally worried about their daughter staying alone in San Jose. Several times, they had indicated that they would help find her a suitable boy to marry. If she were in India, she would have been married by now to a compatible groom, Vijay had jokingly remarked.

Ravi and Neha met each other for the first time during one of the hiking trips to Napa Valley. They met every Saturday thereafter for different hikes around the Bay area and soon their friendship became very close. Both were socially active in Indian festivals like Divāli, Gaṇeśa Caturthi, Holī etc. They also found themselves active participants in addressing global warming issues.

Most of their friends were in their early to mid thirties; more than half were still single; among the married, a few were Indo-American couples.

The hiking group took a four-day trip to the Rocky Mountain National Park. That was when Ravi and Neha knew that they wanted to spend their life together.

They visited each other's family a few times. Vijay and Kavita had instantly liked the young man, charming with a dry sense of humor. They were hoping that Neha would marry him soon. They were very glad he had a similar family and cultural background.

I also asked them about the siblings, as they would be an important part of the wedding ceremony.

Asha was doing her oncology residency in a Chicago Hospital. Ashok and Susan naturally worried about their daughter and hoped that she would find a compatible groom.

Neal was a successful financial consultant in Dallas. His girlfriend, Lisa, was an enthusiastic Yoga teacher and even knew the Gāyatrī (गायत्री) mantra. Vijay and Kavita liked her very much but were not pleased that they were living together without first getting married.

In one of the conversations, Neha mentioned that she would like the best of an Indian Wedding and an American wedding.

Two years earlier, Vijay, Kavita and Neha had attended Kavita's niece, Priti's wedding in Pune, India. They had all enjoyed socializing with their many relatives and friends. Later next year, Neha had also attended her childhood friend Sara's wedding at a Grand Cayman resort in the Caribbean. She shared with us her impressions of those two weddings.

2.2 A Hindu Wedding in India

Neha had always wondered about an "arranged marriage" when her parents had suggested that they would find a very compatible husband for her before she had met Ravi.

When her favorite cousin, Priti, was getting married the traditional way, she traveled to India along with her parents to enjoy the wedding and get to know other Hindu wedding traditions.

The Mutual Selection

Priti was a financial accountant in a multinational company as well as an accomplished Indian classical dancer. After she had started working, it was time for her parents, Kishor and Mrunal, to find a suitable groom for her. No Indian father will ever hand over the responsibility of his daughter to any young man who could not take care of his future family. Of course, it was also important that he came from a similar background in language, culture, religion and even the caste and sub caste. Not only that, he must be well educated and be a physical match to boot. Oh, by the way, their horoscopes needed to be compatible.

Finally, the potential bride and groom had to approve of each other.

After about a year's search through relatives, matrimonial advertisements, and match making bureaus, Kishor's brother in Nagpur suggested his friend's son, Mukul, as a potential match for Priti. Mukul had started his own business of sales and service for digital equipment after an engineering degree from a well-known university. His business seemed well established and the future looked promising. Smart and attractive, Mukul appeared to be a great match as Priti's future husband.

Kishor obtained more information about Mukul and his parents through his relatives. They exchanged photos, horoscopes and more personal information. After a few meetings and with mutual approvals by Neha and Mukul, Mukul's parents dutifully promised Kishor and Mrunal that Mukul had no blemishes and there were no skeletons in their closets at their engagement ceremony. From the time they met for the first time, they would be married in less than six months.

Arranged marriages were common throughout the world until the 18th century. They continue to account for an overwhelming majority of marriages in the Indian subcontinent even though the concept of love marriage is very much accepted and is on the rise. Matchmaking websites try to mimic the principles behind the "arranged marriages" but they lack the experience or mental judgment that parents or other relatives can provide in choosing the appropriate match.

The ancient Hindu literature identifies different forms of marriages based on the way of selection of the bride and groom and its social acceptance by the society. Brāhma Vivāha (ब्राह्म विवाह) is the highest, most appropriate and the most prevalent wedding ceremony among Hindus in modern India. The name may have originated from the belief that Lord Brahmā (ब्रह्मा) performed the wedding ceremony of Lord Viṣṇu (विष्णु) and Goddess Lakṣmī (लक्ष्मी) this particular way. It may have also originated because the Brāhmaṇa (ब्राह्मण), the educated and priestly class, practiced and officiated it.

In this type of marriage, the groom has undergone all the key prescribed Saṃskāras (संस्कार) before the wedding ceremony. He is capable to start and support his future family. The parents and their relatives select the bride and groom based on their compatibility and their own mutual approval.

Mukul had undergone Upanayan (उपनयन), start of education ceremony, when he was eight years old. His Samāvartana, (समावर्तन), the graduation and being ready-to-be-married ceremony, was done just a week before the wedding date.

The Wedding

The auspicious time of Mukul and Priti's Hindu wedding ceremony was 11:45 am on Wednesday, December 26. The next muhūrta (मुहूर्त) was not available until mid April, a very hot season and it would be too long after the engagement! They had chosen this date and the auspicious time based on their horoscopes and for its convenience for the guests. The guests could come at that time, socialize, bless the couple, have a good lunch and go back to their work.

On Tuesday, the evening before, there was Sīmanta Pūjana (सीमान्त पूजन) and a Saṃgīta (संगीत) event, a welcome party for relatives on both the sides. The Sīmanta Pūjana was the formal welcome of the groom and his family to the wedding venue. The Saṃgīta was a song and dance celebration in a very relaxing and informal atmosphere with delicious food.

Vijay reminded Kishor, Kavita's brother, how hard he had twisted his ear at the time of his wedding with Kavita. He told him that he and his family must come to the US for Neha's wedding whenever she would get married in future.

As part of the family, Vijay, Kavita and Neha rushed to the venue early Wednesday morning. Kishor, and Mrunal were busy meeting other family members at the breakfast area that was beautifully set up with a variety of delicious Indian dishes. Many family members were socializing with hearty greetings and laughter.

The paṇḍita had started the Gaṇeśa Pūjā around 8:30 am with the couple and a few family members under a four pillared, decorated canopy called maṇḍapa (मण्डप). The Hindu ceremony involves many different rituals and very few invitees sit through all the steps. The paṇḍita conducts them with the couple and invites other participants as and when he needs them. At about 9:30 am, he called Kishor and Mrunal for a step called Kanyādāna (कन्यादान), literally, a gift of the daughter. In this ceremony, the father of the bride gives away his daughter to the groom and makes him declare that he will never transgress her and his duty towards his family.

After this step, the paṇḍita continued with additional rituals. Neha pulled her chair close to the maṇḍapa where the marriage rituals were happening. The paṇḍita was very learned and could recite all the saṃskṛta verses without looking at any notes. He explained the meanings of the various rituals to the couple in Marāthī (मराठी), the local language.

The origin of the Hindu marriage ceremony is in the Vivāha Sukta of Ṝgveda (ऋग्वेद), the most ancient Hindu Scripture. Written in one of the oldest languages, Saṃskṛta, the ceremony describes the marriage of Sūryā (सूर्या), the Sun's daughter and Soma (सोम), the Moon. It is interesting to note that Sūryā (सूर्या) had bridesmaids and Soma had groom's men! Over next hundreds of years, the paṇḍitas have added verses from other scriptures to the original hymns. In addition, the modern ceremonies include customs and family traditions to create bonds between the bride and the groom and the two families.

The most important steps of a Hindu wedding are:

- Kanyādāna (कन्यादान)- Giving away the bride.
- Kaṅkaṇa-Bandhanam (कङ्कणबन्धनम्)-Binding the couple physically.
- Pāṇigrahaṇam (पाणिग्रहणं)- Promise to stay together
- Maṅgala Sūtra Bandhanam (मङ्गलसूत्र बन्धनम्)-Binding them mentally.
- Vivāhahoma (विवाहहोम)-Worshipping the sacred fire.
- Vastra Bandhanam (वस्त्रबन्धनम्)-Binding them spiritually
- Agni Pradakṣiṇa (अग्नि प्रदक्षिणा)-Circling the fire God.
- Aśmārohaṇam (अश्मारोहणं)-Stepping on the stone.
- Saptapadī (सप्तपदी)-Taking seven vows and

- Saptarṣi-Dhruva Darśana (सप्तर्षि ध्रुव दर्शन)- Praying for a strong marriage.

The paṇḍita completed all the rituals from Kanyādāna (कन्यादान) to Saptapadī (सप्तपदी) by 11:30 am. At this time, the venue was full with more than 500 people. In Indian weddings, all the members of a family are invited, no matter how large. The invitations requested the guests not to bring any gifts or even flower bouquets for the couple.

Priti and Mukul exchanged their clothes with the new ones and got ready for the most important part of the wedding ceremony- the garland exchange with Maṅgalāṣṭaka (मन्गलाष्टक), at the auspicious time of 11:45am.

The Maṅgalāṣṭaka

Priti's māmā (मामा) -her maternal uncle, brought her to the maṇḍapa. Priti and Mukul stood behind an auspicious curtain, each holding a flower garland. After the paṇḍita recited the Vedic Mantras, the guests showered Akṣatā (अक्षता), the auspicious rice grains, on the couple. Then, a group of Priti's relatives recited the "Maṅgalāṣṭaka (मन्गलाष्टक)", a wedding song of eight stanzas. The stanzas were well composed describing the beautiful couple and sprinkled with blessings from the elders. With so many invitees, the guests could hardly see the ritual; they just threw the akṣatā at the end of each stanza in the general direction where they expected the couple to be.

Actually, the maṅgalāṣṭaka is the beginning of the wedding rituals; however, since the relatives recite it at the specific auspicious muhūrta, everybody considers that time to be the only time their presence is required to witness the ceremony and bless the couple.

As soon as maṅgalāṣṭakas were over and Priti and Mukul garlanded each other, all the guests went for lunch, as requested. The paṇḍita continued with Dhruva (ध्रुव) - Saptarṣi (सप्तर्षि) - Darśana (दर्शन), where he asked the couple to pray the North Star for the stability of their marriage and the Seven Stars of the Little Dipper, our seven ancestors, for their blessings. Obviously, it was only symbolic as it was past noon, too bright to see any stars. Alternately, the paṇḍita may ask them to look at the Sun.

After the ceremony, Neha caught hold of the paṇḍita who was more than happy to explain the background and interpretations of each wedding step to her. She really liked the history, depth and spirituality of the Hindu ceremony. She also wondered why this beautiful ceremony was not explained to all and why nobody paid attention to it.

The vegetarian buffet style lunch was very delicious with variety of tastes, aroma and flavors of different spices. There were no formal seating arrangements. In the olden days, there would be rows of chairs and tables and the servers would serve one dish after another, announcing the name of each dish. The hosts urged all the guests to eat more and more even after their bellies were full!

After the wedding, the couple sat in beautiful chairs in the maṇḍapa. All guests came one by one to congratulate and wish them a very happy married life and thanked the hosts for their hospitality.

The last group of people to enjoy the feast was the immediate family on both sides and the married couple. In Indian culture, the hosts will not eat until all the guests have had their meal. Kishor and Mrunal, as the official hosts of their daughter's wedding, were very happy to see so many friends, family, coworkers and friends, young and old, had come to bless the couple.

Vidai (विदाइ)

After the late lunch, it was time to see the newly married couple leave for the groom's home. This is the most heartbreaking event for the bride's family. Priti had lived all her life with her parents and siblings. Now, she had to start a new life with a husband and her new family whom she had met just six months before. Although the marriage is truly a union of two families, it is still hard to let your daughter go to become a part of another family. However, Indian traditions are well established; for one or other reason, the daughter will return home several times, for many well-planned events through out the first few years.

This send off reminds me of what Kanva muni felt, when Śakuntalā was ready to depart his Āśrama to go to King Dushyant's home.

"As Śakuntalā is leaving for her husband's place today, my heart is sinking. Holding back my tears, my throat is choked; I am not able to speak. My eyes blur with worry. With my love for her, my forest dweller's agony is so great, how much grief may befall on poor householders, who send their daughter to her new home?"- अभिज्ञान शाकुन्तलम् - कालिदास

The North Indian weddings that Ashok and Susan had attended in India were similar, except that those started late in the evening and went past midnight.

Then Neha told us about her friend Sara's wedding. Having done some Hindu weddings in similar settings, I could really visualize what she told us.

2.3 A Christian Wedding in the Caribbean

"Gorgeous!" Neha said to herself.

It was a beautiful sunset with a mild breeze along the private beach of the Grand Cayman Resort. Neha was having a mango margarita at the welcome party that Sara and John had arranged for their wedding the next day.

Neha and Sara were childhood friends and grew up together until they finished high school. Sara had moved out of the neighborhood after her parents were divorced but they still kept in touch with each other even after Neha had moved to San Jose.

Sara had been living for six years with her fiancé, John, a divorced father of a young son. They considered themselves married but had decided to formally tie-the-knot for practical reasons.

Their marriage would be called a Gāndharva Vivāha (गान्धर्व विवाह), an older form of marriage that is not legal in India. In the USA, eight states recognize this marriage as legal, a common-law marriage.

In a Gāndharva marriage, the man and woman meet each other of their own accord and consent to live together as a married couple. They consummate their relationship by cohabitation. This form of marriage did not require consent of parents or witnesses, or any rituals to legalize their union.

The most famous Gāndharva marriage in ancient India was that of Duśyanta (दुष्यन्त) and Śakuntalā (शकुन्तला). While on an excursion, the King Duśyanta met Śakuntalā, the daughter of sage Viśvāmitra (विश्वामित्र) and Menakā (मेनका). He saw Śakuntalā in an Āśrama(आश्रम), a hermitage, of sage Kanva (कण्व) and fell in love with her. He and Śakuntalā had a Gāndharva marriage at the Āśrama. Eventually, after many years, Duśyanta formally wed Śakuntalā, who became his queen and mother of his son, Bharata (भरत), after whom the subsequent generations named the Indian subcontinent as Bhārata (भारत).

The Rehearsal Dinner

John and Sara planned their wedding events at the resort on their own with no involvement from their parents. As is customary in the US, they created a registry at Macy's and Nordstrom, where they had listed the gift items they would like to receive from the invitees. That made it easier for the guests to choose a gift that the couple preferred

About sixty friends and family had come to attend the wedding. Many others had declined, as it would have been very expensive for a three-night resort stay and air fare. Although Sara's parents were divorced, each came to the wedding with their respective new spouses. John's parents came all the way from Seattle, WA.

The beautiful resort had a long private beach, a big swimming pool and a wedding venue overlooking the beautiful blue ocean. John had planned the ceremony rehearsal for Friday evening, followed by a welcome dinner.

John had contacted a local priest whom they were going to meet for the first time on Friday to go over the ceremony steps. The couple, their parents and all the bridesmaids and groomsmen gathered at 5:15 pm at the beach venue. Although the Christian Ceremony was going to be only 20 minutes long, the priest went over the essential steps and reviewed all the logistics so that the actual ceremony would be flawless. They rehearsed the groom's arrival, bridesmaids and groom's men procession, bride's arrival with her father, the priest's remarks, Bible reading, ring exchange, vows, unity candle lighting and the recessional.

After the rehearsal, everybody joined for a big welcome party. They all wore Caribbean Party outfits for the evening. This was when Neha enjoyed her favorite mango margarita as the Sun was setting. She also liked the entertainment program of a local dance troupe that the hotel had arranged after the evening dinner.

The Wedding

They had planned the Christian Ceremony for 5:30 pm the

next day. All guests arrived and took their seats by 5:15 pm on the beach chairs. Although it was a private event, there were quite a few hotel guests, in their swimsuits, watching the proceedings from a respectable distance.

Each guest had a wedding program that specified the sequence of events. Right on time at 5:30 pm, the priest welcomed John and his Best Man to the venue, now under an arbor, decorated with fresh flowers. At the priest's signal, the bridesmaids and groomsmen walked to the wedding area through the center aisle, followed by the Maid of Honor and finally by Sara with her father.

The bridesmaids and the groom's men were all dressed in coordinating outfits. All had attended their respective bachelorette and bachelor parties for Sara and John; a few of them would speak at the reception later that evening in honor of the newly married couple.

The priest welcomed the guests and invited all to join in an opening hymn. Then Sara's sister read a passage from the Bible that focused on mutual love between the bride and the groom.

The priest asked the guests if anyone had any objection to John and Sara getting married. With no objections, John and Sara took their marriage vows and declared their commitment to each other. They promised to remain true to each other, in good times and bad times, in sickness and health and to love and honor each other for the rest of their lives. Then they exchanged wedding rings.

There was no tying-the-knot ceremony! It has now become only a figure of speech for a wedding in western culture.

John's mother and Sara's mother tried hard to light their family candles in the evening breeze. The groom's men created a human wall to shelter the candles and that worked! This was the only part that they had not rehearsed the day earlier. John and Sara lit the central Unity Candle indicating joining of the two families with their own union.

The priest declared them Husband and Wife and told John that he might now kiss his bride, which he did promptly.

After the final blessings, the newly wed couple walked down the center aisle with cheers from all the guests and even from some onlookers.

The ceremony was over by 6:00 pm and everybody lined up to take pictures of the married couple as the Sun started setting behind the gentle waves of the Caribbean Sea.

The whole ceremony was well organized, timely and short. The atmosphere was serene and dignified with all paying full attention to the rituals that the priest was officiating. It was little warm in the bright Sun, but still everybody sat quiet through out the ceremony.

Right after some photo shoots, the evening reception started as the sky became dark and stars started appearing in the clear skies. There were speeches by the parents, best man, the maid of honor and a few others. After dinner, the dancing started and the party lasted late into the night.

After returning to her room, Neha had thought, if Ravi ever proposed to her, she would have her dream wedding in the Caribbean.

2.4 Best of Both Worlds

Then it happened on New Year's Eve!

Having seen the two very different weddings, Neha wondered whether she could have best-of-both-the-worlds-wedding to celebrate their Indo-American fusion culture.

Neha and Ravi thought that the wedding should combine the formality, discipline, shortness, schedules, logistics etc. of the modern western weddings and the depth, significance, spirituality and traditions of the age-old Hindu ceremony. They also liked having a destination wedding with only few guests.

Neha wanted to know if Priti's wedding was Brāhma and Sara's was Gāndharva, what her wedding would be called.

"Well, unlike Priti's or Sara's weddings, yours would be a Svayaṃvara (स्वयंवर), a self choice wedding "I replied.

"Can you explain?" Ravi and Neha asked.

In a Svayaṃvara (स्वयंवर) wedding, the bride chooses her own husband, either with or without the approval of the parents. Svayaṁ (स्वयं) means 'self' and Vara (वर) means 'groom'. Another meaning of Vara (वर) is "choice". Still, one more meaning of Vara is best, excellent or choicest. I told Neha and Ravi that they indeed were!

In this form of wedding, on the selected day, the girl garlands the man of her choice and the parents perform the marriage ceremony immediately.

The most famous example of the Svayaṃvara is the wedding of Rāma (राम) and Sītā (सीता). When Sītā reached adulthood, her father, King Janaka, organized her Svayaṃvara with the condition that Sītā would marry only the man who would string the mighty bow of God Śiva (शिव). The sage Viśvāmiṭra (विश्वामित्र) asked Rāma, King Dasharatha's (दशरथ) son, to participate in the contest. Rāma lifted the bow, fastened the string taut and broke the bow in the process. On Vivāha Panchami, an auspicious day, King Janaka performed the Vedic wedding ceremony for Rāma and Sītā.

Thus, in Neha-Ravi' case, although, it was a self-choice wedding, both sets of parents had totally supported their choices; so, we would do the Brāhma Vivāha.

"Best of both worlds" was an excellent objective that all agreed to. However, there were too many options and too many differences of opinions before they could even start planning.

2.5 Reality Check

In America, the bride has a big say in everything that happens at all the wedding events; from the venue selection, the schedule, decorations and even the paṇḍita. As a paṇḍita, my own schedule for the various wedding rituals depends on the bride's schedules for mehndi- a body decoration, her makeup or her photo shoots! "It is my wedding" is a common phrase uttered by many brides around the world but more so in America.

Ravi and Neha had attended a few Hindu weddings in San Jose; those weddings closely resembled the one in Pune. They wanted the best combination of Priti and Sara's weddings. They were not familiar with the manner in which I officiate the weddings; so they had many questions and concerns whether their priest would really do a meaningful ceremony so that their vast circle of American friends would understand the Hindu rituals.

As the bride's parents, Vijay and Kavita wanted to do everything possible to fulfill their only daughter's desires for a beautiful wedding. Soon, they were confronted with many issues like dates, location, venue, logistics, costs, guest lists, which events, relationships, planning and what not.. The weddings that they had attended in India seemed much simpler! They had also attended a few weddings in Houston but did not appreciate all the complexities of the time involved in the planning and the decision-making.

Ashok and Susan also had gone to a few Indian weddings in North India, which were at night and were very festive and colorful. There was so much socializing and merriment that many guests did not even know when the ceremony took place.

All were looking forward to different things! Ashok and Susan, themselves married in the Panjābi wedding traditions, wanted a more North Indian flair to the ceremony. Kavita thought the Maṅgalāṣṭaka (मन्गालाष्टक) was the main part of the wedding but Susan thought it was the Maṅgala Ferās (मङ्गल फेरा). Neha was looking forward to the bridal procession with her grand arrival to the maṇḍapa (मण्डप).

Vijay and Kavita visualized an authentic Hindu ceremony in Houston plus all the traditional events, whereas Ravi and Neha wanted a short but meaningful ceremony at some romantic destination. Both sets of parents wanted a big wedding, attended by their many friends and relatives. However, the couple wanted an intimate celebration with only the immediate family and their close friends.

After listening to the various arguments, Neal suggested that Ravi and Neha should just elope! Vijay even offered to pay the down payment for their future house instead of an expensive wedding. Neha jokingly asked for both! Lisa, who was studying Indian culture, took Neha's side for a lovely Indian wedding.

Neha and Kavita thought that the wedding would be too big and too stressful for them to handle everything. They wanted a wedding planner, who could take a lot off their plate. Vijay and Neal wanted to have a project plan with time line for all activities from beginning to end and thought they could manage all the wedding events on their own.

They shared with me many issues that kept them worried, even though Neha's wedding was supposed to be the most joyful event of their lives. These issues were not unique to them; the vast Indian Diasporas across the world experience them as well.

3. FINDING THE RIGHT BALANCE

Every society, since time immemorial, has faced a generation gap between the old and the young. It becomes much wider and deeper when the first generation is from India and the second generation is born and raised in the western society.

3.1 The Indo-American Gaps

.Starting from the first grade and continuing through high school, the second-generation Indian children become influenced by the American culture surrounding them. After high school graduation, they leave their home to attend college elsewhere, which makes them independent and self-confident. Yet, they struggle to balance their values and traditions taught at home with attitudes and practices that are more prevalent in the western culture. They try to find their own identity, mixing with students with similar backgrounds; yet being a part of the western society they are brought up in.

The Hindu culture in America has seen remarkable growth since the 1970s. There are Yoga studios, temples, philosophical and spiritual centers and Indian restaurants in every major city. This growth has significantly increased the positive image of Indian culture among Americans.

After their children settle in their professions, it is very natural for their parents to bring up the subject of their marriage as they feel more comfortable after their sons or daughters are married and well settled. Some children may agree if the parents want to introduce them to prospective leads but in general, they are not very comfortable with the concept of arranged marriage. The first generation Indian parents may not have much choice but hope that their culture will prevail in their choice of their future spouse.

Most first generation Indians have been financially successful in America. With their previous modest backgrounds in India, they tend to be fiscally conservative. However, when it comes to their daughter's or son's wedding, they celebrate it with great enthusiasm and spend a lot more money than their American counterparts do. Even then, they tend to be very value conscious. The second generation may be more extravagant to their taste.

Most Indian parents are also socially conservative when it comes to dating and marriage in the more liberal American society. They themselves got married by the traditional "arranged" marriage system. They prefer that their daughter or son marry someone with a similar background. They want to preserve their own culture and pass on their traditions to their grandkids. The

Hindu philosophy states that the marriages of children are essential to repay the parents' debts to their own parents, to facilitate rebirths of departed souls and continue the family heritage.

Thus, it is natural for first generation parents to worry about their children's choice of their spouse. They worry that they and their grandchildren may totally lose their own culture; more so, if they marry a non-Hindu person.

The American vs. Indian societal statistics, at this time, support that view. However, one should remember that, about 100 years back, American families were much stronger than they are today. America may be just ahead of rest of the world in terms of these changes in family structure.

Today, in India, the rate of arranged marriages is almost 90%. In 2012, 74% of respondents in a survey conducted in India approved of arranged marriage and preferred it to freely chosen marriage. In American society, that statistics is probably close to zero. American parents probably do not feel getting their children married is a part of their responsibility unlike in India.

Back in India, more than 90% of Indians in the 25-35 year old category are married compared to less than 50% of Americans. India has a much larger percentage of married householders, about 90%, compared to about 50% in America. The multi generational households comprised about 50% of the households in India whereas they are less than 10% in America. The older generation still commands more respect in India; less so in the western countries. For most couples in India, it is their first and probably the last marriage unlike in America, where it may be a second marriage for either bride or the groom and they may even have children from the previous marriage. After the wedding of their children, the bonds between the two Indian families remain strong with frequent communications and genuine relationships; they are much weaker in corresponding American families.

The American values are trickling down to second generation Indians in the western countries; more single people, more divorces, less understanding of Hindu culture and breakup of the family units. India is also changing towards similar statistics, slowly but surely. In every society, old cultures disappear, replaced by new ones. That is the way it is.

Some couples live together before officially getting married. This really worries the Indian parents who wonder the rationale of a formal Hindu Wedding. They advise their children to get married by a civil ceremony before cohabitation. Many couples indeed do that. I have not signed marriage certificates for about 50% of the couples; because they already had a previous certificate.

With the couple and parents as the two legs, the third leg of the triad, the Paṇḍita, can help these weddings with a pragmatic approach by treating them as what they are, a celebration of the bride and grooms' union with their friends and family. It is worth it if he or she can inject some Hindu philosophy into their future married life. These weddings can be a true fusion of not only the eastern and western cultures but also of different faiths and races.

Most non-Hindu brides or grooms prefer to get married only by a Hindu Ceremony. They find Hindu traditions and culture to be more liberal, inclusive and pragmatic compared to their own faiths that may be more restrictive and dogmatic

I have performed a few weddings jointly with Christian priests. However, a time constrained single fusion ceremony may not do full justice to either culture. Many couples choose two separate ceremonies to celebrate their wedding with the customs, traditions and philosophical views of marriage of each religion.

Thus, it is important for the couple and their parents to choose a Paṇḍita who understands the intercultural, intergenerational and interfaith gaps and works with them for a meaningful wedding. This triad is the key to a successful wedding.

3.2 The Role of the Paṇḍita

The paṇḍita is not only an officiant but also a consultant, an advisor, a problem solver and a negotiator. With his or her years of experience, he or she can effectively guide you to plan the religious events and advise you about other issues.

Some parents prefer the professional paṇḍitas who have learnt the intricate rituals of all Saṃskāras and Pūjās. They may follow the same procedures, as they would back in India with some modifications. They perform all rituals (कर्मकाण्ड) per the scriptures with outstanding recitals of saṃskṛta mantras. Many of them also explain the meaning and philosophy (ज्ञानकाण्ड) of the wedding ceremony to the couple and guests. However, a full-fledged ceremony can be too long and too regional to allow any flexibility for couples from for other regions of India. If not well communicated, it can become tedious giving opportunity to guests to socialize.

Paṇḍitas associated with organizations as Āryā Samāja (आर्य समाज) and Jñāna Prabodhini (ज्ञान प्रबोधिनी) perform simpler and shorter versions. They explain the ceremonies in the local, understandable dialects to all the attendees.

Then there are paṇḍitas who are primarily interested in the study of Hindu philosophy as prescribed in our scriptures. They perform the Vivāha and other saṃskāras, not as a profession but more to convey the wisdom of our ancestors and as a service to the community. They tend to be more philosophical than ritualistic. Their ceremonies are relatively short but meaningful. They may be professors, engineers, or scientists in other fields but with a good understanding of Hindu philosophy and its contributions to a stable society.

In India, the bride and the groom are mostly from the same Varṇa (वर्ण) or caste and from the same region. However, in western countries, the brides and grooms have mostly different regional and cultural backgrounds. Although some common threads exist, the rituals and traditions from Kaśmira to Kanyākumāri and Rājasthāna to Āsāma can be significantly different. Therefore, the paṇḍita needs to explain the various options based on their own culture and then customize the religious events that are consistent with the desires of both parties.

My experience with interfaith weddings has been largely positive. Most Christian parents are delighted to be a part of the Hindu ceremony. However, in a few cases, they may be apprehensive about participating in Hindu rituals. The paṇḍita should be proactive to remove any concerns they may have. The paṇḍita should be flexible enough to include some Christian or Jewish steps, if needed. After the wedding, the non-Hindu participants should have a more positive impression of our culture than they had before.

The paṇḍita needs to communicate effectively during the planning stages as well in performing various rituals. We do have accents; so, we need to speak slowly and clearly. He or she needs to be in command with appropriate measures to make the ceremony interactive, serene, formal, seamless, and still complete it in an hour or so. In essence, he or she must connect to the audience.

It is obviously essential that he or she be well versed in saṃskṛta language and chanting of mantras associated with various rituals. However, he or she should do the ceremony mostly in English with sprinkling of only few key mantras for the authenticity. More breadth than depth works well for the Indo-American audience.

The ceremony can be more interesting if the paṇḍita can inject some humor into the ceremony; but not jokes! The wedding atmosphere should be serene but still a few, well delivered one-liners can get some key points across and make the ceremony lighter and Lively.

The paṇḍita can demystify the ceremony by explaining it, not as a series of discrete and independent steps but as a sequential story of the couple, from their first meeting to a very happy wedding. The paṇḍita should also ensure a good logical, sequential and positional flow for all involved in the ceremony. The paṇḍita should pay attention to the overall set up of the maṇḍapa and the hall for good sound and visibility.

The traditional Hindu wedding is a dialogue between the various parties such as the bride's father, the bride and the groom, as directed by the paṇḍita. Many paṇḍitas do this dialogue themselves on behalf of them. It is more authentic if the couple and the parents actually speak the specified words and sentences instead of just saying "I Do" or nothing at all.

The paṇḍita needs to adapt to the changing roles of the bride and the groom. The Hindu ceremony has not changed much since the Vedic times. We have been conducting the same rituals for thousands of years even though the demographics of the society and the marrying couple have changed significantly. For example, some rituals indicate a subordinate role of the bride as if the groom is inducting her into married life. Concepts such as the Kanyādāna - gift of the bride or Saptapadī- Follow me- etc. need to be modified in today's' context. The ceremony must reflect the equal but complementary roles of the bride and groom, better interpretation of various steps and respect for their individual aspirations.

The paṇḍita should also be familiar with the legal requirements of his authority to sign the marriage certificate. The laws vary from state to state and even from county to county. For example, in Texas, any paṇḍita can sign the certificate as long as he conducts the ceremony per Hindu religion and the parents and the couples accept him as their officiant.

Finally, the paṇḍita should plan for a rehearsal a day or two before the ceremony with all key participants. He or she needs to be proactive in this regard. At the rehearsal, it is important to go over the logistics and timings, explain the rational of key steps and review any last minute changes to the program.

By bridging the various gaps, the paṇḍita can really help the families plan a very pleasant journey, from engagement to the wedding celebration.

3.3 Bridging the Gaps

On Valentine's Day, Ashok and Susan responded enthusiastically to Neha's idea of a Caribbean wedding. It would be even better, if it could be in February! All Vermonters would love to get out of the cold weather for a few days! However, Vijay and Kavita were non-committal.

They soon discovered that there were many other differences between the two generations, two cultures, and two families and even between men and women on both sides. They really needed to address them right at the start.

Auspicious vs. Practical Time

Kavita had called me because she wanted Neha to get married on an auspicious day and time, the Muhūrta (मुहूर्त), as per the

Hindu calendar.She had already given up looking into whether Neha's and Ravi's horoscopes matched. An auspicious Muhūrta for the wedding was the least that she wanted. Ravi and Neha did not understand, nor could their parents explain to them what it was and why it was so important.

Ravi and Neha wanted their wedding on a Saturday since most people love to attend the joyous occasions over a relaxing weekend. Vijay thought Sunday was a good option as many venues offered reduced rates and hotels too had lower rates for accommodations. However, that option did not go well with the couple. One thing that they all agreed on was not to have a wedding around popular holidays like Memorial Day or Labor Day due to heavy traffic.

Having conceded that the wedding would happen on a Saturday, Kavita wanted to know which Saturday morning would have a good Muhūrta.

With logistics, weather, convenience and venue availability plus a Saturday wedding as primary considerations, I thought it was impractical to look for a Muhūrta too. I advised the family to do the ceremony at the most logical time but, if possible, avoid Rāhu Kāla (राहु काल),which happens every Saturday morning. I personally do not understand why this particular time is inauspicious other than it is named after Rāhu, a demon planet who was believed to cause eclipses of the Sun and the Moon which are considered inauspicious events. In general, Hindus consider darkness as sign of ill omen, ignorance, laziness etc.

They were looking for a Saturday in March next year. The Hindu lunar calendar, Páñcānga (पञ्चाङ्ग), stated that, on March 9, the Rāhu Kāla would be over by 11 am plus minus a few minutes depending upon the exact location. Any time after that would be fine for the ceremony.

Morning or Evening Wedding

Neha preferred a morning wedding and evening reception to give all ample time between the two events. On the other hand, Neal thought that a morning ceremony would add significant lunch costs for 300 guests. Further, an afternoon wedding followed by reception would flow more smoothly with a relaxed morning after the Saṃgīta the previous evening. Nobody had to hurry in the morning for the baraat and the women did not have to wake up early for their make up. The locals did not have to make two trips to the venue either.

"We also do not have to worry about Rāhu Kāla!" Vijay observed.

However, Neha and Kavita pointed out that there would not be much time between the ceremony and reception for the photo shoots and for them to get ready for the reception if the wedding was in the afternoon. In any wedding, women rule; so this eventually got resolved in the women's favor.

Local vs. Destination

Having decided the date, they started looking for a suitable venue.

Vijay and Kavita, being very practical, wanted the wedding to be in their hometown, Houston. They knew a number of good venues within a reasonable distance from their home. Houston would be a great choice for guests who would be flying in from many US and international cities. The weather would be nice in early spring. The wedding would also be less costly than doing it anywhere else.

Ravi and Neha were thinking of a beautiful destination wedding; a scenic area like the Rocky Mountains of Colorado- that was where they fell in love- or still better, a beach resort in Cancun, Mexico- Neha's as well as Vermonters' favorite. They wanted their wedding to be memorable, a once in a lifetime experience for all.

I have officiated many weddings at many beautiful seaside resorts. These resorts have great beaches, a variety of restaurants, many swimming pools and great indoor facilities. All resorts have special packages, especially for weddings, where everything is included - all meals, drinks, resort activities and outings to nearby attractions. The evening cocktail receptions under starlit skies are beautiful with the resort's own exciting entertainment, like the local fire dances.

Therefore, yes, a destination wedding would be a memorable experience for all attendees. However, they soon discovered many impracticalities of a Cancun or Colorado wedding. They dropped Colorado, as it would still be too cold in early March; not a huge draw for the Vermonters.

For a Cancun wedding, they would have to make a few trips to plan the events and carry many items from Houston. Just imagine the baggage fees the parents, the couple and the guests have to pay, carrying multiple outfits -from formal to beach clothing and all the wedding paraphernalia! In addition, the resort accommodations would be expensive for many guests. Neha had experienced that at Sara's wedding, where many of her friends could not afford to go. She did not want that unlike the wedding she knew about where the hosts used un-affordability of a destination wedding as a screen to minimize the number of guests!

Neal was also concerned about the extra expenses of taking all their relatives from India to Cancun. They also found that there were no Indian vendors in Cancun as good as those in Houston.

Finally, they dropped the idea of a Cancun wedding. Ravi and Neha were disappointed but they knew it was the right thing to do. The Vermonters too were disappointed but they were glad that more would attend a Houston Wedding, still in warmer weather, with many sightseeing options and good affordability.

Self-Management vs. Hire a Wedding Planner

Initially, Kavita was overwhelmed with too many issues to consider and was not sure whether they could handle all the tasks. Neha, being in San Jose, did not think that her parents alone should carry all the burden of planning and event management. However, once they decided to do the wedding in Houston, Vijay felt very comfortable, as he had handled many work projects with critical paths, tight schedules, various dependencies, costs pressures and tight deadlines. Neal was a value oriented financial consultant and was more than willing to fulfill that role.

Still, they decided to hire a wedding planner, Julie, to minimize their workload, reduce their own stress and allow them to spend more time with their guests. The wedding planner can be a very helpful asset, especially during the hectic times of the various wedding events. Julie specialized in Indian weddings and with her years of experience and negotiating skills was able to help them choose the venue and other vendors.

Outdoor vs. Indoor

Once they decided to do the wedding in Houston, Ravi and Neha still were eager for a romantic outdoor setting.

In the old days in India, most weddings were outdoors. Our Hindu Culture worships nature and it is quite appropriate that we celebrate the wedding in the beauty of Nature. Outdoor environment is also great for socializing, welcome parties and even for the reception with colorful evening skies and mild breeze.

The outdoor venues can give you more flexibility in choosing vendors and can be less expensive relative to a four star hotel. However, they do have many constraints for an ideal wedding.

In Houston, the early March weather would be pleasant but it could still be too cold, too hot, too sunny, rainy or windy. Lighting the holy fire would be a challenge even with the slightest wind. Neha remembered this problem at Sara's wedding when they tried to light the unity candles. She also remembered that the audio system had not worked well because of the constant buzzing sound of the wind. A late morning to mid afternoon ceremony would be out of the question because the overhead Sun would make everybody very uncomfortable, even if it were not too hot in early March.

Some other venues like a historic building, an arboretum or a park had other drawbacks such as limited availability and inadequate facilities for a large gathering. Very few outdoor venues provided a stage for the maṇḍapa, which was important for the bare feet ceremony and good visibility. None of them had rooms for out of town guests; so one may need to arrange transportation at extra cost.

Therefore, they all agreed to have an indoor wedding at a nice hotel. Still, they had multiple choices with plusses and minuses of each.

Prestige vs. Value

Although Ravi and Neha were again disappointed, they did realize a good hotel in Houston was the best overall option for all their events.

The high-end hotels that Neha preferred would have been 20-30% costlier with no added benefit other than their prestige and name recognition. They would have been too expensive for some guests. Neha suggested offering an additional choice of a more affordable hotel. However, Vijay observed that this situation would really create bad optics plus transportation issues.

After looking at a number of four-star hotels, they settled on a suburban Marriott that seemed excellent for all the wedding events and accommodations. The nightly rates were reasonable enough so they themselves could stay in the hotel for four days to enjoy the events without having to run around between different venues. The hotel also offered big suites to the parents at a significant discount and complimentary honeymoon suite for the couple. There were no parking fees or traffic issues, normally associated with downtown hotels.

Couple's vs. Parents Guests

The guest list was a big sticking point between the couple and parents. Each of the parents had a large number of relatives and friends in the US, Canada, England and India. Neha and Ravi had their own big circle of friends from all over the US. They did not understand why they had to invite their parents' relatives and friends they hardly knew for *their* wedding. However, for the parents, it was a great opportunity to invite them for the big event in their lives.

They all trimmed their lists reluctantly to come up with a reasonable number of about 300 guests. Vijay and Kavita had the toughest job of deciding whom to invite locally being in Houston for so many years.

Ravi and Neha had no qualms about sending an electronic invitation to their friends. The parents decided to send formal invitations, printed in India. Vijay and Kavita also decided to deliver the invitations personally to their relatives and friends in town. They all agreed that they should centralize the RSVPs at the wedding website only.

Traditional vs. Modern Ceremony

"Would you do the ceremony in English? Would you explain the meaning of every step?" Ravi asked me in one of the early phone calls.

The ceremony would be mostly in English with explanation and significance of each wedding step. We would also take into consideration customs and traditions from both families.

"By the way, can we skip Kanyādāna (कन्यादान)? We are not *giving* away our daughter to the groom!" Kavita asked.

Many brides' parents and the brides themselves do not like the literal meaning of Kanyādāna (कन्यादान); physical gift of the bride to the groom. I personally see this as "giving away the bride in marriage", an act of marrying her to a suitable groom with approval of the bride and all family. Parents and brides have suggested many alternatives to the word Kanyādāna. The Paṇḍita can modify it as giving permission for the groom to marry the bride.

Having attended Priti's wedding, both Kavita and Neha thought that the Hindu ceremony treated the bride inferior to the groom in many respects. I assured them that I would modify many of these steps to reflect the equal but complementary nature of today's couples.

"Can we do the ceremony in 30 minutes?" Neha asked.

It is interesting that many brides have no problem sitting

two-three hours for their mehndi or make up or hairdo. However, they are not hesitant about asking to curtail the time for the most important event of their wedding. They ask this question because they have attended Hindu weddings that were too long and boring.

Over the years, I have concluded that I can complete the key rituals within an hour provided there is a full logistics review of an agreed program. Inadequate planning, no logistics review, dress changes and gift giving during the ceremony, unnecessary additions of regional customs and doing every ritual in detail are some of the causes of long and tedious ceremonies.

"Can we add some western traditions like the personal vows and ring exchange?" Susan asked.

"Sure!" I replied.

In addition to Karavlis (करवली), the bride's and groom's helpers, in this case Priti and Asha, Ravi and Neha planned 10 bridesmaids and 10 groomsmen for the bridal procession. They were pleased that it would be an hour long, serene and formal ceremony with all essential rituals.

Interfaith Weddings

The second-generation young people may not have any issue with dating or marrying non-Hindus. My own data indicates that more than 50% of second generations Hindus choose a non-Hindu as their spouse. The couples themselves need to resolve many issues related to marrying a person of different faith. Some Indian parents may not approve of the interfaith or interracial weddings but eventually they do come around.

The website InterfaithShaadi.org is an excellent source to discuss those issues prior to tying the knot. The primary issues discussed on that website are related to lack of respect and equality for the other religion, possible conversion, in which faith to raise their children, etc.

Doing pre wedding rituals, as described later, is especially important for interfaith weddings, as the non-Hindu bride or groom can benefit highly from this open and informal discussion. We need to bring forth our all inclusive and non-dogmatic culture in a non-proselytizing way.

Whether Hindu or non-Hindu, the most important criteria must be the attitudes and culture of the person you or your son or daughter wants to marry. Secondly, we need to trust our children that they will make the right choice for their own well-being.

Many a time, the couple prefers Hindu ceremony alone with some western features as readings of love poems or readings from the Bible. I am more than glad to accommodate those requests.

Pre Wedding Saṃskāras

The wedding events are one of the important instruments to strengthen the Hindu family values, which include the duties and obligations of the four stages of life. The Vivāha Saṃskāra is the last saṃskāra that the parents do for their sons and daughters; so it is an excellent opportunity to promote our culture so that the new couple instills those values in their own children.

Ravi and Neha were planning only the Mehendi, the Saṃgīta, the ceremony and the reception. Ashok and Susan wanted to do pūjā (पूजा) before the wedding. All of them had heard about some other pre wedding rituals but none had any idea why one did them or why they were important.

It took a few discussions before they all understood that the Brāhma Vivāha is not just an hour-long event but it is the final destination of years' long journey involving many saṃskāras along the way. These saṃskāras are part of a continuous life cycle, a microcosm of Hindu philosophy and are essential to preserve the Hindu way of life. The Vivāha Saṃskāra is the most important rite of passage; it integrates the past, present and future generations vertically and connects the two families horizontally. In addition, it ties together the four objectives of human pursuit as related to the four stages of human life as will be explained later.

Normally, the groom's and the bride's parents do separate

pūjās in the morning just before the wedding. However, that is a very busy time for all; so, I advise both sides to complete all pūjās a day or two before.

They decided to do the Upanayana (उपनयन) and Samāvartana (समावर्तन), to mark the beginning and end of educational periods, respectively for Ravi and Neha. Then the parents would do Vāgdāna (वाग्दान), the formal wedding commitment.For practical reasons, they decided to do Grahaśānti (ग्रहशान्ती)-pūjās for various deities- by the two families together, at the hotel, instead of separately in their own homes.

Both parents realized that doing these pre wedding rituals was one way to bridge western and the Indian value gaps and pass on their own traditions to the next generation. Ravi and Neha agreed; still not fully grasping their importance.

It took them a couple of months to formulate the main plan for the wedding. Now, the time had come to discuss additional items.

Regional Differences

Various states of India have different languages, history, culture, attire, food and traditions. There are different ways of doing the same rituals; the sequence may vary from region to region, yet, the common Sanātana Dharma holds all that together with emphasis on the key objectives of Hindu life.

Ashok was from the northern state of Panjāba (पंजाब). Susan had gone to India several times and had attended a few Panjābi weddings. Vijay and Kavita were from the western state of Mahārașṭra (महाराष्ट्र). In a Mahārașṭrian ceremony, they hold a curtain in between the bride and the groom until the auspicious time; whereas in Panjābi ceremony, the bride may receive the groom as soon as he comes with the Baraat. Mahārașṭrian weddings have only four circles around the sacred fire; Panjābi ceremonies may have seven. Panjābis introduce their respective relatives, just before the wedding but the Mahārașṭrian do it a day earlier. Ravi would wear a Sehra, the traditional headdress whereas Neha would have a Mundāvali, a face ornament.

There are similar differences in every wedding where the groom and brides are from two different parts of India. The paṇḍita should accommodate those differences as much as possible with rationality and flexibility.

Vegetarian vs. Non-Vegetarian Menu

Ravi and Neha had recently become vegans along with many of their hiking friends. They considered being vegan was healthy, was good for the planet and showed respect to all living beings. They were glad that the acceptance of a plant-based diet was growing.

Vijay and Kavita were vegetarians. Ashok, Susan and Neal occasionally ate chicken and fish at restaurants. Many Americans and Indians would prefer meat dishes at the reception. They could have added a meat dish to the menu; but all agreed that it was best to serve vegetarian meals at all functions, nodding to the desires of the marrying couple.

Another sticking point for the reception was whether they should have a buffet dinner or a sit-down plated dinner; the latter considered more formal, more upscale but also more costly. Ravi and Neha preferred the plated dinner; but realized that it would be more efficient to serve a buffet dinner.

Likes vs. Dislikes, Right vs. Wrong

There were differences of opinion in many other aspects of the wedding. What should be the criteria to resolve them?

Everybody has likes and dislikes; but each should also consider what is right and what is wrong , say, from an environmental or health or cost perspective. Somehow, Ravi had embraced this thought! He was able to convince Neha that whenever there was any conflict, they should decide what would be best for the environment, which in most cases also lowered the discretionary expenses. This helped them make such decisions as not to have fresh flower bouquets on every table at every event.

Complementing Different Views

Any marriage signifies the union of two people who complement each other in all aspects of their lives. This becomes very important during the planning stages when men and women express different views of various wedding aspects. It is best that they compliment each other in bridging those different views.

It was time to fine-tune each aspect of the wedding.

3.4 Planning for Perfection

Bridging those multiple gaps between various parties significantly reduced everybody's stress level and gave them a clear path to plan all the events. Vijay, Kavita, Neha and Ravi visited me in Austin to work out further details. Neha also wanted to show Ravi the University of Texas and meet many of her local friends.

Planning the Events at the Venue

Vijay and Kavita had now started enjoying the journey to the Big Day. The wedding was in their hometown. They were getting all the necessary help from their local friends, wedding planner, hotel manager plus my two cents.

They had chosen the upscale suburban Marriott hotel for all their wedding events. The hotel had various capacity function rooms, ample guest rooms, dining facilities and a big, beautiful ballroom for the main events. They even allowed them to cater Indian food from outside vendors. The guests did not have to go to multiple locations for different events; thus, there were no guest transportation issues.

The hotel was well equipped with all the facilities for large gatherings. The function rooms had built-in audio systems, tables, chairs, stage and other equipment as needed. The lobby was big enough to receive the Baraat, the groom's arrival procession, and do the welcome ceremony.

They were able to visit the hotel multiple times, at any time of the day. They were surprised how many trips they made to the venue to make sure that they worked out the minutest details! In one meeting, the hotel manager became very concerned when he heard about "the fire" and first wanted extra money to cover insurance and fire marshals. Over the last 25 years, this issue has become not as bad as it used to be. After I showed him how small the fire would be, he agreed to have his own safety person during the wedding with a fire extinguisher, just in case.

Creating a Manageable Schedule

Any wedding is a big social celebration! Therefore, it is best to spread out all events with enough slack time so that the hosts and the couple themselves have enough time to socialize and enjoy the events themselves. Therefore, they made multiple adjustments to the overall schedule.

Saturday morning would be too hectic, as all would be getting ready for the ceremony, so we moved Gouri Har (गौरी हर) Pūjā, normally done just before the wedding, to Thursday afternoon. Ashok and Susan moved Milani (मिलनी), the meeting of respective family members from each side, normally done before the ceremony, to Friday evening. Susan decided to do the Chūda (चूडा) - putting on the bangles- ceremony for Neha Friday morning. They also decided to do her Gṛha Praveśa (गृह प्रवेश), welcoming bride to her new home, not at the hotel, but later, when she would come for the first time to their home in Burlington.

We settled on the logistics review or rehearsal for Friday late morning; thus keeping Friday afternoon free for Vijay and Kavita to meet and greet the arriving guests and prepare for the evening welcome Saṃgīta.

Vijay and Kavita made a key decision to move to the hotel Wednesday evening; that allowed them to start events Thursday morning in a relaxed manner. They also planned for a hospitality room from Friday to Sunday mornings where guests could enjoy breakfast, tea and coffee.

Creating a detailed schedule is one thing, but adhering to

it during the busy wedding events requires great discipline. I have had many events starting late for very avoidable reasons. The hosts, couple and guests all benefit from adhering to the planned schedule. This is where the wedding planner can be a big help.

The wedding planner, Julie, spent a lot of time identifying the pinch points. She made sure that there was adequate time for all the vendor preparations, photo shoots, mandap set up, women make ups, flipping the ballroom, speeches etc; so that every event would start and finish at predetermined times.

Communicating and communicating well

With all events in Houston at one location, it made it much easier for Vijay to meet local vendors personally to resolve many issues.

Ravi and Neha planned a wedding website with information about the venue, guest accommodations, event schedules, town attractions, expected weather etc. They also included their own personal information about when, where, how they met and how Ravi proposed to Neha. They also included short descriptions about parents, siblings and all bridesmaids and groomsmen.

They wrote an overview of all the wedding events. They answered the following most important questions that Americans ask about a Hindu weddings

- What can you expect at each event?
- What is the dress code at each event?
- What are the suggestions for gifts, if any?

They decided to state "No Boxed Gifts" which really meant "Cash" which was probably the most practical gift.

A good website can help all the invited guests, especially those, who may not be familiar with the Hindu Culture. Neha kept its contents current, accurate and consistent throughout the planning process.

Planning the ceremony Rehearsal

"Do we really need a rehearsal?" Kavita asked in one of the

phone calls.

Many Indian parents are reluctant to allocate their precious time for the rehearsal; they think it is unnecessary, as they all know what to do since they have attended many similar weddings.

In India, a rehearsal for the ceremony is not required since there is no time constraint or formality. However, in the western environments, the ceremony needs to flow smoothly, be relatively short and must be well coordinated among many participants. It involves many steps that need good explanations to the couple and to the guests. A simple procedure like tying a knot or putting a necklace on the bride can take precious time and create unnecessary confusion. We do not stop the ceremony for the "right" photo angle!

The rehearsal is much more critical for an interfaith wedding as there can be many questions and/or apprehensions on the part of non-Hindus participants. The paṇḍita needs to meet all the people involved in the ceremony so that he or she can review their roles and answer any questions. The rehearsal is also a logistics review of all the critical steps that make the wedding ceremony well coordinated, on schedule and seamless.

Adapting Best of Indian and American Ceremonies

Neha was very much relieved when I told her the wedding ceremony would promote the best of American and Indian ceremonies; the formality, and discipline of Sara's wedding and the depth, traditions and spirituality of Priti's wedding. I assured her that the ceremony would reflect equal but complementary roles of the bride and groom.

The western concepts of the bridal procession and ring exchange have become normal traditions at all Hindu weddings. In addition to the Hindu scriptural vows, some couples write their own personal vows as well, per western tradition. I have also included some specific readings at the requests of American brides.

There have been very few issues at the interfaith ceremonies that I have officiated. In fact, many non-Hindu participants were pleasantly surprised with the depth, history and spirituality of the ceremony.

Making it an All Inclusive Ceremony

The parents, the bride's and grooms' siblings, other family members and guests have important roles to play in the couple's wedding. Their strong and supportive roles are extremely important for the future success of the couples' marriage. They all are witnesses to the ceremony; they bless the couple when they take the marriage vows and formally induct them into the second stage of life of married householders, the bedrock of any society.

Hence, in addition to the couple, this wedding ceremony would require participation of parents, the siblings, aunt and uncle, the bride's- maids and groom's men and the guests.

Assuring Good Visibility and Good Acoustics

With an open maṇḍapa on a stage, the ceremony is very visible to the large number of guests. The paṇḍita needs a clip on or head microphone; the latter has a better and consistent sound quality.

Neha and Ravi planned the background music and special songs at the arrival of the groom, arrival of the bride and some final boisterous music at the end of the ceremony.

Creating Enough Backups

A project plan must also have back up plans for critical aspects of the wedding. Vijay had chosen highly reliable local vendors for all activities. The Marriott hotel had experience with multiple Hindu weddings. The early March weather had a good historical record. I also asked Vijay to make sure that he knew another available priest who could fill in as my back up.

While planning for a perfect wedding, one should always remember the Murphy's Law: If any thing can go wrong, it will! So, plan for all possibilities!

Finalizing the Big Plan

Vijay and Kavita also needed to focus on other events like the Saṃgīta and reception. Ashok and Susan took over the responsibility for planning the Saṃgīta. Of course, the younger generation had a major say in deciding every detail!

Julie completed the project plan by the end of September with every detail spelled out.

- Wednesday Evening - Hosts move to the hotel
- Thursday Morning - Haladi for Ravi and Neha
- Thursday Afternoon - Pre-wedding rituals for both families
- Thursday Evening - Mehndi
- Friday Morning - Chūda and then Rehearsal
- Friday Evening - Saṃgīta & Dinner
- Saturday Morning - Wedding Ceremony and Lunch
- Saturday Evening - Cocktail Reception and Dinner
- Sunday Morning - Farewell Brunch

Not all weddings have all these events! I have officiated many wonderful weddings just with an afternoon ceremony followed by reception. This wedding is an example to describe the typical events associated with an Indian Wedding.

From September to March, the couple and parents were busy sending invitations, going to India for shopping, food tasting, planning trips for overseas guests, hiring photographers, DJs, beauticians and what not! The time passed quickly.

Before they knew, it was the Thursday before the wedding.

4. STARTING THE EVENTS

Do we need to do earlier Saṃskāras (संस्कार) before the wedding?

In Sanātana Dharma, the parents perform the saṃskāras-sacraments or the rites of passage, for their children, to develop their physical, mental, spiritual and intellectual upbringing. These saṃskāras, from conception to Vivāha, create a solid foundation for the lives of married householders. Indeed, the education period from Upanayana, the start of the education until Samāvartana, the graduation from the chosen field, determines the success or failure of their children for the rest of their lives. Hence, it is better late than never to do these saṃskāras before the wedding, if the children have not undergone them before.

Nowadays, many parents do not perform all the saṃskāras, except the Vivāha, or even if they did, celebrate them as social functions rather than instill their true purpose in young boys and girls. In case of this particular wedding, the parents and the couple wanted to understand the fundamentals of these saṃskāras.

4.1 Early Saṃskāras

Vijay, Kavita, Neha and Neal had moved to the hotel Wednesday evening; so did Ashok and Susan. They kicked off the wedding events Thursday morning with a separate Haladi for Ravi and Neha. The primary intention of Haladi, (हलदि), smearing them with turmeric paste- was to purify their minds and beautify their bodies prior to their wedding. It also turned out to be a fun event for all of them as well as for their relatives.

They scheduled the saṃskāras and pūjās from 1:00 pm to 4:00 pm in the afternoon. Vijay had booked a big room at the hotel for about 75 friends and relatives. This is the first time I met Ravi's parents Ashok, Susan and his sister, Asha. As promised, Neha's māmā, Kishor had travelled from India along with his wife Mrunal, his daughter Priti and her husband Mukul. I was also glad to meet Neha's older brother, Neal and his girl friend, Lisa.

All had removed their shoes outside the room, as they respected that room as a sacred place for the saṃskāras and the pūjās. Once inside, it was important that everybody was physically comfortable to focus on the rituals. Therefore, Kishor had arranged chairs for all guests, unlike normal Hindu tradition of seating on floor. He planned the event on a stage for good visibility. They would not serve any food during the rituals to keep the sanctity of the occasion.

Ever since Vivekananda gave his address at the Chicago Religious gathering in 1892, there has been a growing understanding all over the world of Sanātana Dharma (सनातन धर्म), an eternal way of right living for all human beings. The best way to reiterate that understanding is through interactive discussions with the attendees. This works especially well with non-Hindu guests.

Learning essentials of Sanātana Dharma (सनातन धर्म)

After greeting all, I initiated a discussion on the name of our religion. Most people thought it was Hinduism; eventually, somebody gave the correct answer as Sanātana Dharma.

Pre Vedic civilizations practiced Sanātana Dharma on the banks of river Sindhu (सिन्धु) in northwest India. Hindu is a corrupted, geographical designation for people following Sanātana Dharma. The British coined the word "Hinduism" only recently, around 1830 CE. It is not a religion like Islam or Christianity with a specific founder, known start date or dogmatic beliefs based on a single book. It is an eternal, broad, pragmatic, all-inclusive way of living and an amalgamation of many different philosophies. It sustains all Creation- human beings, animals, plants and material elements. It upholds everything through the natural and cosmic laws of the Universe. The primordial hymns- the four Vedas (वेद) and the main 108 Upaniṣadas (उपनिषद्) - are its bedrocks.

After this introduction, I asked how many Gods were in Sanātana Dharma. The answers varied from 330 millions to 33; eventually somebody correctly answered as One.

There is One and Only God-Brahman (ब्रह्मन्), an all-pervasive Supreme Being who is both immanent and transcendent, both Creator and Unmanifested Reality. Brahman is the source of all creation, animate and inanimate, is changeless, timeless, attribute less and formless. It is the total existence, consciousness and bliss; Sat-Cit-Ānanda (सत्-चित्-आनन्द). It is the material and efficient cause of everything in the Universe.

Moreover, our own Ātmā (आत्मा), our soul, is a fraction of that Brahman. There is Only God, here, there, everywhere. Creator and Creation are the same.

ॐ, एकाक्षर परमब्रह्म। एकं, अद्वितियम् ॥ एकं सत् , विप्रा: बहुधा वदन्ति॥

"Om is the only (one) God, none second. There is only one Being, people call It by different names"

We relate to Brahman through different deities with different names, different forms, different attributes and different duties. Therefore, we have deities for creation, maintenance, dissolution, wealth, prosperity, long life, knowledge, children, etc.

Brahman is an abstract concept, too difficult to explain in a short time. Therefore, I give an example of our Sun as one of the manifestations of Brahman; total energy and the source of all life on Earth. I ask them to think of their cell phone as the body with all attributes like seeing, hearing, talking, remembering etc and its battery as Ātmā, which derives its energy ultimately from the Sun. This analogy makes it simple to explain oneness between Brahman and Ātman.

With folded hands, we all prayed to Śrī. Gaṇeśa.

"वक्रतून्ड महाकाय कोटि सूर्य समप्रभ। निरवीघ्नं कुरु मे देव, सर्व कार्येषु सर्वदा॥"

The wedding ceremony would be a transition for Neha and Ravi from the first stage to the second stage of their lives as per the Āśrama (आश्रम) System.

According to Vedic philosophy, our Ṛṣis (ऋषि) divided the human lifespan into four stages known as Āśramas. Āśrama is an educational, philosophical and spiritual hermitage, somewhere in the forest or on the bank of a river. In the context of human life, it means a stage or a period of life, associated with a specific activity. The four stages of life are the Brahmacharya (ब्रह्मचर्य) - the student life, Gṛhastha (गृहस्थ) - the married life, Vānaprastha (वानप्रस्थ) - the retired life and Sanyāsa (सन्यास) - the spiritual Life.

The first stage, Brahmacharya Āśrama, starts with Upanayan. It is the student phase of life when the boy or the girl studies the skills that will earn his or her livelihood in the next stage of life. It ends with Samāvartana- the graduation.

The second stage, Gṛhastha Āśrama, starts with the wedding. It encourages the enjoyment of a material life and natural desires with the right way of living. The householders raise their children, give them a solid educational foundation and teach them their religious, spiritual and social duties.

The third stage, Vānaprastha Āśrama, starts with retiring from the active life of the householder. It literally means spending this stage of life in the forest hermitage. It focuses on minimizing material possessions, being mentors to the younger generation and serving society.

The fourth stage, called Sanyāsa Āśrama, starts with the renunciation of material possessions. One spends his or her time in meditation and the spiritual contemplation of the meaning of Life and the Universe.

Upanayan (उपनयन)

I normally perform Upanayana when the boy or the girl is around 10 years old. At this age, he or she can grasp key aspects of this sacrament.

"जन्मना जायते शूद्र, संस्कारै: द्विज उच्यते।" Everybody is born in the lowest human caste; it is only with all the Saṃskāras, he or she is reborn to achieve the full potential of all his or her faculties.

According to traditional Hindu culture, the children should have undergone the Upanayana and Samāvartana, before being eligible for their wedding. Vijay had undergone both and his son, Neal, had undergone only Upanayana. None of them understood the underlying significance of the ceremony. Vijay was surprised when I said that Neha should have also undergone these Saṃskāras On the other hand, Ravi's father, Ashok, told me that it was not a tradition in their community.

There is a general belief that only the boys and those too only from the Brāhmaṇa (ब्राह्मण) class are eligible for the Upanayana Saṃskāra. That is not true; anybody, who goes to school for study, whether a boy or a girl and from any background, is eligible.

Unfortunately, this pragmatic approach is still not widely accepted, even in India. I recently did the Upanayana for a ten-year-old girl but her grandparents declined to attend the ceremony. The fact that the sacrament did exist in the Vedic period and was later replaced by the wedding itself, did not change their minds.

In Upanayana, the father initiates his son or daughter into the student life, which is a life of chastity and pursuit of knowledge. He also binds them into a strict code of conduct -Vratabandha (व्रतबन्ध), which will be very conducive to whatever discipline he or she wants to pursue.

Student Code of Conduct

At this time, I asked Ravi and Neha what were the most important things that they followed to concentrate on their studies.

"Avoid all the distractions!" Neha replied.

Yes, we call that as controlling the senses to focus on studies. In addition, eating nutritious, healthy food, doing proper and regular exercise, self-study, homework and helping others, are the essential behaviors, which students should observe for an excellent education during the student life.

Education is a top priority among all Indians in the United States. Finding the best school district is very high on their list of priorities when they decide to look for a house. One can see the successful results of that priority in various fields such as engineering, medicine, business etc.

Many Hindu scriptures exalt the importance of knowledge in different ways. Here is a verse from the Gītā (गीता).

"न हि ज्ञानेन सदृशं पवित्रं इह विद्यते॥ (Gītā 4.38)"

"There is nothing more sacred than the pursuit of knowledge."

Taittiriya Upanishad says:

"सत्यं ज्ञानं अनन्तं ब्रह्म॥"

Brahman is the Truth, the ultimate and limitless knowledge.

Whereas the Mundak Upanishad says:

"सत्यं एव जयते, न अनृतं ॥"

Truth alone conquers or prevails, not untruth.

Yajñopavītam (यद्न्योपवितं)

A second essential element of the Upanayana Saṃskāra is wearing of the sacred thread called Yajñopavītam (यद्न्योपवितं). Its three strands have multiple meanings. The one who wears it should be pure in thought, word and deed. The strands also represent the endless Cycles of Creation, Preservation and Dissolution, through the trinity of Gods, Brahmā, Viṣṇu and Śiva. Our own life is a cycle of birth, growth and death and again rebirth, growth, and death and so on. Everything that we observe in Nature is cyclical; the days, the seasons, photosynthesis, water and being part of Nature, we too are cyclic.

The knot in the middle of the sacred thread represents the formless Brahman, the pure form of energy, which pervades the entire Universe. Everything in the universe emerges from and then merges into Brahman.

Hindus also believe in the Law of Cause and Effect- the Karma (कर्म) - by which each individual creates his own destiny by his thoughts, words and deeds; we then experience consequences of our actions. The ultimate objective of his life is Mokṣa (मोक्ष) - the realization that God and its Creation, including himself or herself, are the same. All life is sacred, to be loved and revered, and therefore one should practice Ahiṃsā (अहिंसा), practicing non-violence, physically or mentally.

Gâyatrî Mantra (गायत्री मन्त्र)

Earlier, Vijay and Ashok had studied the Gâyatrî Mantra and recited it at least a thousand times so that they would be eligible to teach it to their children and explain its meaning to all the guests. Both did a superb job in reciting it and explaining its significance to Ravi and Neha.

The Gâyatrî Mantra is the supreme mantra, revealed to sage

Viśvāmiṭra, who wrote it in Ṛgveda.

"ॐ भू:। ॐ भुव:। ॐ स्व:। ॐ मह: । ॐ जन: । ॐ तप: । ॐ सत्यं।
तत् सवितु: वरेण्यम्। भर्गो देवस्य धीमहि। धियो यो न: प्रचोदयात् ॥"

"We meditate on the glory of that Sun (The manifested Brahman), who is worthy of our worship. He may inspire our Intellect."

After Ravi and Neha recited the Gâyatrî Mantra, Vijay tied a band around Neha's waist and Ashok did the same around Ravi's waist. The waistbands would remind them the student code of conduct to follow in their student lives.

Ravi and Neha symbolically left to their Guru's Āśrama to pursue their studies as guests blessed them for a successful student life. They returned to the hall within a couple of minutes having completed their twelve years of education.

Samāvartana (समावर्तन)

The graduation ceremony prepares the young man or woman for the next stage of life. At this time, we release them from the student code of conduct and they receive atonement for any misdeeds. Here is the updated set of instructions from various Upaniṣadas (उपनिषद्) that the teacher gives to his disciples at graduation and then they are ready for a married life.

- Know that Brahman is the ultimate and limitless knowledge.
- Always speak the Truth. Truth alone conquers or prevails, not untruth.
- Follow your own Dharma. Dharma will protect those who protect Dharma.
- Non-Violence is the ultimate Dharma.
- Never give up on Self Study and do listen to Discourses.
- Always do your prescribed duty the Right Way.
- Treat your mother, father, teacher and guest equivalent to Gods.
- Donate with humility.
- See the goodness, hear the goodness and speak the goodness

to everybody, everywhere, every time.

- Eat nutritious food and exercise for healthy body.
- Protect the Earth. She will protect you.
- Do not take unnecessary risks, as you will be responsible for the wellbeing of your family.

We now call the groom Snātaka (स्नातक), an initiated householder, and the bride, Saubhāgya Kānkshiṇī (सौभाग्यकाङ्क्षिणी), one who brings good fortune. After the wedding, the married couple will perform these saṃskāras on their future children. Thus, the life cycle continues from one generation to the next.

4.2 Pre Wedding Rituals

Vāgdāna (वाग्दान)

The two families had an engagement party on Valentine's Day the year before. However, they did not have a Hindu engagement ceremony per our saṃskāras. This ceremony is called Vāgdāna (वाग्दान) which means giving a verbal promise for a future wedding, by the bride's and groom's parents to each other.

So, why should they do this ceremony now, just before the wedding, when they had already celebrated the engagement a year before? Well, we do it for following reasons.

- First, Vāgdāna is according to Brāhma Vivāha tradition.
- Second, it is the start of the formal joining of the two families and,
- Third, we introduce the couple the key objectives of human life.

During vāgdāna, the two families make sure that the future bride and future groom are very compatible with each other and there are no skeletons in anybody's closet! Only after they are fully satisfied, the parents give their word to each other for a future wedding with full funfair.

In Hindu marriage, the bride has all the essential qualities. We worry only about the groom! Therefore, Vijay and Kavita made sure that Ravi met the following criteria.

"He was not arrogant, ignorant, or insane. He could support a family. He was willing to get married. He was healthy. He was not striving for Mokṣa now! He did not travel too much. Finally, he was not forgetful because it was important that he would remember what his future wife would tell him to do!"

Then I explained to Ravi and Neha the objectives of human life, the four Puruṣārthas (पुरुषार्थ).

Artha (अर्थ) is food, shelter, power, security, material wealth, etc.; Kāma (काम) is your physical and emotional desires. Artha and Kāma are common to all living beings. What separates human beings from the rest of the animals is the pursuit of Dharma and Mokṣa (मोक्ष).

Dharma is striving for stability and order, for a life that is lawful and harmonious. It teaches us to do the right thing, be good and virtuous, be helpful to others and uphold the Natural and Cosmic laws. Mokṣa is the striving for the Liberation from life-rebirth cycles and Self-realization, the Spiritual understanding of 'Tat Tvam Asi- तत् त्वं असि'- that Ātmān and Brahman are the same.

During the wedding ceremony, the couple commits to pursue Dharma, Artha, and Kāma. The primary duty of householders is to raise a family with safety, security and well-being while following the right way of living. Mokṣa is an individual pursuit after fulfilling all the duties of householders."

After making sure that there were no skeletons in each other's closets and having made sure that Neha and Ravi understood the human life objectives, Vijay and Ashok committed to their wedding; just two days from now!

After a short break, it was time to do Grahaśānti (ग्रहशान्ती), the prayers to various deities and heavenly bodies.

Grahaśānti (ग्रहशान्ती)

Normally, the two parents perform Grahaśānti separately, in their own homes, a few days before the wedding. However, there are a few advantages of doing them together at the venue. The joint Pūjā strengthens the bonds between the two families; more relatives are able to attend the rituals and both families gain the same understanding of its deep significance.

During Grahaśānti (ग्रहशान्ती), Hindus propitiate various heavenly bodies and the surrounding Nature to remove their potential adverse effects on the future lives of the couple.

We cannot survive without the Five Big Elements- पञ्च महाभूतानि - the Earth, Water, Fire, Air and Space. Hence, we started the pūjā s by first worshipping our own planet, Pruthvi (पृथ्वी), the mother Earth, a living and breathing planet. But she is hurting because of human blunders that have caused extinction of many species and created pollution, deforestation and global warming. Ravi and Neha immediately understood the wisdom of our culture that respected the Big Five Elements.

Then, we worshipped the Dikpālas (दिक्पाल), the directional guardians. Our ancestors did not carry any insurance for life, home or car; instead, they prayed to the deities of various direc-

tions to protect them from unexpected events that could hit them from any direction. Hence, they worshipped the deities, which they believed to be the guardians of each of the ten directions.

1.East- Indra, Lord of the celestials. 2.South East -Agni, the Fire deity. 3.South-Yama, God of Death & Justice. 4.South West - Nirṛti, the Demon 5.West-Varuna, the Water Deity.6.North West- Vāyu, the Air Deity.7.North- Kubera, Gods' Treasurer. 8.North-East- Śiva, the Dissolver. 9.Up -Brahmā, the Creator.10.Down-Viṣṇu, the Maintainer.

Our ancestors had observed that the Sun, Moon, Mercury, Venus, Mars, Jupiter, and Saturn were moving counterclockwise against the fixed stars. They also believed that there were two other unseen planets, Rāhu and Ketu, which caused eclipses of the Sun and the Moon.

We absolutely cannot live without our own planet Earth. However, sometimes, it can affect us adversely with earthquakes, volcanic eruptions and floods. Similarly, we are very dependent upon the Sun for light, energy and heat, but it can create adverse weather like too much heat, tornados and hurricanes.

Our ancestors also believed that one's fate or destiny depends upon the positions of these planets at the time of one's birth, the Horoscope. Therefore, we request these heavenly bodies to give their blessings and remove all potential difficulties in the bride and grooms' married lives.

Among all the heavenly bodies, the planets Maṅgala (Mars), Śhani(Saturn), Rāhu and Ketu are believed to be more inauspicious and to affect one adversely. We also have a 10th planet, which may cause big troubles for the bride's family.

So, who is that 10th inauspicious Graha?"Jāmatā Dashamo Graha (जामाता दशमो ग्रह:)"It is the future son-in-law!

Graha Yajña (ग्रहयज्ञ) or Grahamakha (ग्रहमख)

Agni is the Vedic fire god in Hinduism. He is also the guardian deity of the southeast direction. In Vedic literature, He exists at three levels, on earth as fire, in the atmosphere as lightning and in the sky as the Sun. This triple presence connects Him as the messenger between Gods and human beings. Hence, we invoke the various heavenly bodies with oblations to Agni.

Mātṛka Pūjā (मातृका पूजा)

As a part of the Grahaśānti (ग्रहशान्ती), we worship all the Goddesses, who are the true powers behind the Gods. Without their power, none of the Gods can fulfill their duties; which is also true in the human and animal kingdoms.

Nāndī Srāddha (नान्दी श्राद्ध)

Hindus believe in Saṃsāra (संसार), the concept of rebirth and cyclicality of life. We stand on the shoulders of our ancestors. Every living creature is in debt to those who came before it. It tries to repay that debt by helping the dead being reborn and continuing the next life cycle. For Nāndī śrāddha (नान्दी श्राद्ध), we pay homage to their ancestors and request their blessings for the marrying couple.

Maṇḍapa Devatā Pūjana

We do this pūjā is to assure the success in the creation of the auspicious maṇḍapa and to assure that all rituals in the maṇḍapa happen successfully without any problems. We worshipped six goddesses who are the guardians of the four corner and two central posts of a traditional maṇḍapa.

नन्दिनै नमः। नलिन्यै नमः। मैत्रायै नमः। उमायै नमः। पशुवर्धिनै नमः। शस्त्रगर्भायै नमः।

Gaurī Hara Pūjā (गौरी हर पूजा)

Pārvatī (पार्वती), Umā (उमा) or Gaurī (गौरी) is the Hindu goddess of fertility, love, beauty, harmony, marriage, children, and devotion; as well as of divine strength and power behind Śiva. She is also the reincarnation of Sati (सति), Śiva's first wife, who had entered a sacrificial fire after her father had insulted Śiva. It was Pārvatī who wooed Śiva, also known as Hara (हर) for their eventual marriage. Pārvatī and Śiva are often symbolized by a yoni (योनी) and a linga (लिङ्ग) respectively. The combined icon represents the interdependence and union of feminine and masculine energies in creation and regeneration of all life.

Normally, only the bride worships Gaurī and Hara for an eternal marriage and children. In today's environment, both Neha and Ravi did this Pūjā.

Vijay and Kavita formally invited all deities to attend the wedding events. After Śrī. Gaṇeśa Ārati, Susan and Kavita did an Aukṣaṇa (औक्षण), wishing Ravi and Neha very healthy and long lives.

Vijay concluded the pre wedding rituals with thanks to all participants. The evening Mehendi program was mainly for the women. It was the first evening for all the relatives to meet and mingle. It was a fun and social evening for all!

4.3 The Day Before

The most hectic day for the parents and the couple is the day before the wedding ceremony, Friday in this case. There are so many guests to welcome; vendors to talk to and countless, last minute, little things to take care of. Therefore, it is best to keep this day relatively free to minimize the stress on everybody. However, the rehearsal and the logistics review had to be on this day because almost all participants would be present and it would be at the venue.

Logistics Review

We all gathered for the rehearsal at 10 am at the ballroom where the wedding would take place the next morning. The parents and the couple had reviewed and approved the program. Kavita had done a great job designing it by selecting the right font and its size for the program to be readable, even in dim light. Neha and Ravi had added a nice thank-you note to all the guests for attending the wedding and giving their blessings.

We started the rehearsal with an overview of the ceremony as a story.

- The groom and bride come to the maṇḍapa, separately, symbolizing their separate lives. They approve each other with a garland exchange.
- The groom asks permission from the bride's parents to marry their daughter! After extracting a promise that he will always be faithful to her, the father joins their hands and "gives away" his daughter.
- The bride and groom request each other to fulfill their individual duties and desires for their future married life and promise to stay together forever. The couple seals their marriage with three different knots.
- The couple requests Agni, the Lord of the Home, for a long and happy married life. While circling around the sacred Fire, the groom describes their complementary relationship. The couple takes seven vows for a healthy and prosperous life.
- After the priest declares them as husband and wife, the guests bless them for a successful married life.

We reviewed all the key steps from arrival of the groom to the final departure of the married couple from the maṇḍapa. . We rehearsed some key rituals, which needed detailed explanations and which could be time consuming if not coordinated well. Ravi had no idea about how to tie the Maṅgala Sūtra around Neha's neck! Neither did Asha and Priti know how to tie the wedding knot!

The couple and the parents were required to recite some

Saṃskṛta mantras. We rehearsed a few lines along with their meaning.

Ashok wondered whether Neha could greet Ravi right after the baraat as was the custom in North India. I told him it would take away from her dramatic entry to the maṇḍapa later.

Ashok and Susan were still not comfortable that there would be only four Ferās (फेरा). Their own wedding had seven! I briefly explained to them that going around the sacred fire had an entirely different significance than the seven vows with seven steps. We would do those separately.

Ravi also wanted to know whether they could play the finding-the-ring game that Ashok and Susan had played at their wedding. It would cause logistic issues and extra time; he quickly dropped that idea. However, Priti wanted to play stealing-the-groom's-shoes game.

In traditional ceremonies, the groom's parents have no specific role. However, I involve them in multiple ways. The groom's parents accept the bride after Kanyādāna, symbolically, through the waterfall. The groom's father lights the fire for Vivāhahoma. Later, they accept her after the Ferās as a part of their family. Ashok and Susan were delighted to know that!

Ravi and Neha had chosen a beautiful open maṇḍapa on a big stage with steps on either side and in the front center. Since there would be a large number of guests at the ceremony, they were also going to set up two side video monitors.

After resolving all their questions, I reviewed the seating arrangement for the couple and the parents and showed them where all the items would be. The area in front of the couple would be completely free for all the rituals. Bride's parents, siblings, and the bride would enter the stage from the left side; groom's parents, groom and his siblings enter the stage from the right side.

All participants entering the maṇḍapa must remove the shoes. I also requested Mrunal to remove the deities from the maṇḍapa right after the ceremony; because many guests would surely enter it with their shoes on for the photo shoot. As is the Indian custom, there would be tea/coffee and snacks outside the wedding hall for the guests before the ceremony starts. Julie would make sure that nobody would take any snacks or drinks inside.

There is always a question regarding where the wife sits relative to her husband! It really depends upon the occasion. In social situations, she is on the left; in religious occasions, she is on the right side of her husband. So, during the wedding ceremony, she is on the right side of her husmabd.

Looking towards the maṇḍapa, the groom's side was on the right; the bride's side on the left. They reserved first few rows for immediate family members, the bridesmaids, and groom's men. There would be no photographers coming on the stage during the ceremony, taking all their pictures from a respectable distance.

I use a gas fired smokeless Agni Kuṇḍa (अग्निकुण्ड) or Havan Kuṇḍa, the Sacred Fire Pit, that is portable with a flame controller on/off valve. I made sure that the ceiling above the maṇḍapa was high enough so that any unexpected smoke or heat will not trigger any alarms.

It is better to conduct most rituals with the parents, the couple and the paṇḍita in standing positions. This simple act shows great respect for the rituals, makes them very visible to all the attendees and is great for photographers. The paṇḍita should be heard from the side; not much seen in the center.

Some parents want additional people in the maṇḍapa. More people can cause more distractions! Therefore, it is best to limit them to the parents and the couple. In addition, the parents should avoid chatting among themselves or with their relatives in front chairs, during the ceremony

We also reviewed the different music that Ravi and Neha had chosen for the different parts of the wedding ceremony. Mrunal reviewed her recital of Śrī. Gaṇeśa prayers and Maṅgalāṣṭaka.

After the rehearsal, the parents and the couple felt very much relaxed, knowing that the ceremony would go as per the program and on time.

Saṃgīta

The evening Saṃgīta started at 6:30 pm with milani (मिलनि) - the traditional introduction and greeting of respective members from each family. I was afraid that somebody might fall down as each tried to lift the other up in a real competitive spirit; fortunately, nobody did. This is when I met John and Sara, the Gāndharva couple, who had tied their knot in Grand Cayman. They were both glad that Neha had decided to marry in Houston instead of in Cancun. Even though it was a small wedding, it proved to be lot more challenging than they had expected.

I was also happy to meet Maya and Ryan, the Indian-Chinese-Scottish couple whose knot we had tied a few years back in Dallas. This time, both wore Indian outfits; Maya in a beautiful sari and Ryan in a silk sherwani. I told them that it was at their wedding that I connected Celtic "Tying the Knot" tradition to the Hindu wedding of binding the couple with various means, physically mentally and spiritually. Ryan was delighted to know his own ancestral tradition. He remarked how it so closely resembled the

Hindu tradition.

Then, I met Asha, Ravi's younger sister, who introduced me to her colleague, Dr. Paul Caswell. Paul had accompanied her to attend his very first Indian wedding. Soon Asha had to rush, as she was the master of ceremony for the evening along with Neal, Neha's older brother.

The program started with all the old timers, led by Vijay, Kavita, Ashok, and Susan, danced to their favorite old Bollywood songs. Priti's classical Kathakali dance was one of the highlights of the evening. The hiking group from San José, with their cowboy hats and western outfits delighted the audience with their rendering of Rocky Mountain High. They knew that it was in the Rocky Mountain National Park where Neha and Ravi knew that they would marry and live together forever. Then Lisa, Neal's girlfriend, played "Jai Ho", the Oscar winning song, on her flute to a standing ovation.

Neal and Asha managed the timing well so that all songs, dance routines and speeches were over by 10 pm. This was critical as the bride and all the women needed to get up early for their hairdos and make-ups for the Big Day.

5. CONDUCTING THE CEREMONY

We got up early Saturday morning to prepare for the big day. Soon, it was time for all of the guests and the groom's side to head to Baraat and for me to go to the maṇḍapa to set up all the required items at their appropriate places.

5.1 The Physical Connection

The Groom's Baraat and Welcome

The joyous procession of Ravi and his family started on time at 10:00 am. Ravi rode on a decorated horse while the DJ played some lively songs to get the folks dancing. Many guests from the bride's side had joined the fun as well.

Vijay and Kavita welcomed Ravi, then Ashok and Susan, then Asha and the rest of the groom's family with Madhupark (मधुपर्क), a mixture of honey and yogurt. All the guests were treated to Mango Lassi and some snacks for the enthusiastic dancing they had done bringing Ravi to the venue. Julie made sure nobody took the snacks inside the wedding hall.

After all the guests took their seats, Vijay and Kavita escorted Ravi, Ashok and Susan to the maṇḍapa. They all took their shoes off and somebody discretely took Ravi's shoes away. As they sat, I showed them various items that they would need during the ceremony and then we waited for a few minutes for the Rāhu Kāla to be over at 11:15 am.

Starting the Ceremony

I welcomed all the guests to the auspicious event with a brief introduction of the Vivāha Saṃskāra. I recited the famous verse how the bride's family chooses her future husband.

"कन्या वरयते रूपं, माता वित्तं, पिता श्रुतम्। बांधवा: कुलं इच्छन्ति, मिष्ठानं इतरे जना:॥"

It says that the bride chooses a handsome groom, mother wants him to be rich, father wants him well educated and the relatives look for a good family.

Ravi was happy that Neha considered him handsome; Kavita showed some disappointment that Ravi was not very rich,

Vijay was happy with his education. Ashok and Susan smiled when Vijay's relatives approved of them as having a great family background! However, the guests broke into laughter when I told them that they were there only for food and drinks!

Not true. The guests were witnesses and they needed to bless this lovely and joyous union of the bride and the groom. It was with their blessings and strong support; that their marriage would be healthy and everlasting. I asked them to focus on the various rituals, be active participants and be witnesses to this union.

Kanyā-Āgamanam (कन्या आगमनम्)

As soon as I announced the arrival of Neha, Neal and Mukul came to the maṇḍapa and held the auspicious curtain, the antar-pata (अन्तर्पट), in front of Ravi. Julie coordinated the arrival of Neha, with the two karvalis, flower girls, bridesmaids and groomsmen, with melodious background music.

Neha's māmā (मामा-maternal uncle), Kishor, who had been declared as his sister, Kavita's guardian at her wedding, 33 years back, escorted Neha to the maṇḍapa. At that time, he had twisted

Vijay's ears to remind him to take good care of Kavita. Now, it was his solemn duty to bring her daughter, Neha, to her wedding having fulfilled his role.

Ravi had not seen Neha since the Saṃgīta; so he very much wanted to see her arrival, but Neal and Mukul held the antarpata high.

Ravi's had worn a classical turban with Sehra, whereas Neha had the traditional Mundāvali on her face.

Ravi and Neha stood across from each other, holding garlands in their hands. The antarpata indicated their separate existence until this moment; two bodies, two minds and two souls. This ceremony would remove all obstacles and inhibitions and unite them together, physically, mentally and spiritually.

Mrunal, Neha's aunt, had prepared a Maṅgalāṣṭaka, an auspicious song that poetically offered blessings to Neha and Ravi. As she recited the Maṅgalāṣṭaka, Neha and Ravi focused internally and thought about the journey they were about to undertake as a married couple. The parents showered the couple with flowers at the end of each stanza. The guest's turn would come later.

After Neal and Mukul removed the antarpata, I asked Neha and Ravi to look at each other very carefully! This step is Vadhu-Vara-Parspara-Nirīkṣaṇam (वधु वर परस्पर निरीक्षणम्). I asked them to make sure that each one wanted to spend the rest of life with the other person!

They indicated their mutual approval by garlanding each other; Neha first, as she had chosen Ravi to be her future husband, as per the Svayaṃvara tradition.

Śrī. Gaṇeśa Prārthanā (श्री गणेश प्रार्थना)

Mrunal recited an invocation to Shri Ganesh, the God of wisdom and remover of all obstacles. All guests held their hands in prayer position to request His blessings for the success to this ceremony.

Puṇyāhavācana (पुण्याहवाचन)

According to Hindu traditions, the parents are the prime drivers for their son's or daughter's wedding. This is the last Saṃskāra they perform to induct them into the married life. They emphasize its objectives, which are to lead their lives in the Right Way, following Dharma and continue the next life cycle with progeny.

Each of the parents proclaimed those objectives for their son and daughter.

"आवां कन्यायाः (पुत्रस्य) धर्म प्रजोत्पादन सिद्धीद्वारा, श्री परमेश्वर प्रीत्यर्थं, विवाह संस्कार करिष्यावहे।"

All Hindu weddings happen on an auspicious time based on the couple's horoscopes and the planetary alignments. However, there is also an alternative! The parents and the honored guests can declare this wedding day to be auspicious and the ceremony to be fruitful in every way: This is Puṇyāhavācana (पुण्याहवाचन). It is another wonderful way to involve all the guests to be a part of the ceremony.

All the guests repeated after me that let this day be auspicious, let the wedding events complete successfully, let there be a long and healthy life for all and let there be peace everywhere.

"ॐ पुण्याहं। ॐ स्वस्ति। कर्म ऋध्यतां । शान्तिः अस्तु। पुष्ठी: अस्तु।
तूष्ठी: अस्तु। आयुष्यं अस्तु। आरोग्यं अस्तु। ईष्ठ संपदम् अस्तु।"

Saṃkalpaḥ (संकल्प)

The Hindu wedding ceremony is a spiritual, emotional, religious, legal and a social commitment by the bride and the groom, to each other first, to their parents, to their spiritual Gods, to their ancestors and to all their friends and family. By committing to Artha, Kāma, Dharma and following a Spiritual Life, they bring stability, continuity, prosperity and happiness, not only to their own lives but to the future generations as well. The Gṛhastha Āśrama they enter is the real backbone of all societies and that of other Āśramas.

I asked Neha and Ravi to declare their intention to get married, having approved of each other and understood the objectives of married life. They jointly declared the following Saṃkalpaḥ (संकल्प) - their marriage resolution in Saṃskṛta.

"इह पृथिव्यां, अमेरिका राष्ट्रे, Texas प्रान्ते, Houston ग्रामे, अध्य, विलम्बि नाम सन्वत्सरे, उत्तरायणे, फाल्गुन मासे, शुक्ल पक्षे, तृतीया तिथौ, शनिवासरे, रेवती नक्षत्रे, आवां गृहस्थ आश्रम स्वीकार पूर्वक, धर्म, अर्थ, काम सिध्यर्थं, विवाह संस्कार करिष्यावहे।"

They repeated the same resolution in English as well, so that they would always remember this most important day of their lives.

"On this Planet Earth, in these United States, in the state of Texas, in the city of Houston, at the Marriott Hotel, today, Saturday, March 9th, Hindu year 1941, at 11:35 AM, we commit to enter the second phase of our lives, the lives of householders. We do this, in order to pursue Dharma, Artha, and Kāma."

All the guests proclaimed "तथास्तु।" which meant let it be so!

Kanyādāna (कन्यादान)

Although Ravi had asked Vijay's permission to marry Neha about a year earlier, he had to do it again now, in front of all family and the guests.

In a Svayaṃvara, the groom has to prove that he is a worthy suitor for the bride, competing with hundreds of other eligible bachelors. Rāma had to lift the mighty Śiva Bow and string it. Arjun had to hit the eye of a rotating fish on the ceiling by looking at its image in boiling oil on the floor. What had Ravi done to win Neha over?

Not knowing, I asked Vijay and Kavita whether they were sure that Ravi was the most worthy suitor for their beloved daughter. They looked Ravi over, discussed a few things among themselves and after a some time, what must have appeared as an eternity to Ravi, said "Yes."

In the Brāhma Vivāha, the bride is Lakṣmī (लक्ष्मी) and the groom is Viṣṇu (विष्णु). By entrusting Neha's future to Ravi, with all deities as witnesses, Vijay and Kavita hoped to repay their own debts to their ancestors by continuing the next life cycle. They said to Ravi:

"कन्यां कनक संपन्नां कनका भरणै: युताम्। दास्यामि विष्णवे तुभ्यं ब्रह्म लोक जिगीषया।
विश्वंभर: सर्वभूत: साक्षीण्य: सर्व देवता:। इमां कन्यां प्रदास्यामि पितृणां तारणाय च।"

Then Vijay joined the right hands of his daughter, Neha and Ashok and Susan's son Ravi, with an objective for them to pursue Dharma. Artha, Kāma,

"अशोक च सुषमा च पूत्राय, रवि नामने वराय, मम पूत्रीम, नेहा नाम्नीम् कन्यां,गृहिणी
पद स्वीकार पूर्वकं, धर्म, अर्थ, काम सिध्यर्थं तुभ्यम् अहं सम्प्रददे।"

Ravi said to Neha that it was with love that he would accept her hand in marriage. "कामेन त्वा प्रतिगृह्णामि।"

Then he promised her parents to follow the right way of living and to continue the next life cycle with progeny.

"धर्म प्रजा सिध्यर्थं कन्यां प्रतिगृह्णामि।"

However, that was not enough! He had to promise Neha that, while pursuing Dharma, Artha and Kāma, he would always remain faithful to her.

Ravi said to Neha "धर्मे च, अर्थे च, कामे च, न अति चरामि त्वया अहम्। "

Just to make sure that he would always remember this vow, he repeated it twice more.

In the old scriptures, women were always assumed faithful to their husbands. However, they all worried about the men! Therefore, during the marriage ceremony, only the groom needed to promise that he would remain faithful to his future wife. Well, in the spirit of equality and mutual respect, it made sense that Neha should also promise Ravi that she would remain faithful to him as well.

Hence,Neha too promised Ravi that she too would remain faithful to him.

"धर्मे च, अर्थे च, कामे च, न अति चरामि त्वया अहम्। "

In philosophy as well as in rituals, we consider life as a cycle. Water is life, with its eternal cycles, is created and recreated from one generation to the next. Thus, the waterfall from mother to daughter through the father and the groom and future mother-in-law represents the natural life cycle.

Kavita poured water from the kalasha (कलश), a small pitcher, on Vijay's to Ravi's and then to Neha's joined palms. Susan collected it in a bowl as a sign of acceptance. Ashok dutifully handed towels to Vijay, Neha and Ravi.

Kaṅkaṇa-Bandhanam (कङ्कण बन्धनम्)

Facing each other, Neha and Ravi tied each other's wrists with the sacred thread. This Kaṅkaṇa Bandhanam represents a physical knot. The couples tie this knot after the father joins their hands and the couple commits to Artha - physical assets like home, security, safety, money etc and Kāma - physical fulfillment for procreation. These two are the major objectives of all living beings.

5.2 The Mental Union

Akṣatāropaṇam (अक्षतारोपणं)

In Indo-American weddings, the bride and groom know each other for a long time. They are very good friends and never run out of things to talk about subjects of their mutual interest and future married life. Nevertheless, physically and mentally, God created men and women very differently. In addition, they have different aspirations and different expectations from married life with their own separate careers.

A well-known book says, "Men are from Mars, Women are from Venus." How true! Mars rotates anticlockwise, Venus rotates clockwise and they orbit on opposite sides of the Earth.

In the old days, whether in India or in the US, women looked after the household chores and welfare of the family whereas men provided for their food, shelter, safety and security. That traditional model is long gone. Ravi was an engineer; Neha was a lawyer, each with different goals and aspirations. Therefore, it was very important that they recognize, respect and help each other in fulfilling those goals and aspirations. Mutual respect, open and free communication and allowing each other to grow in their married life are the most important ingredients of marital success. This is Akṣatāropaṇam.

First, Neha requested Ravi to fulfill her wishes for her married life.

"भगः मे कामः समृध्यताम्। श्रियः मे कामः समृध्यताम्। प्रजा मे कामः समृध्यताम्॥"

Neha wanted him to fulfill her wishes to be very happy, wealthy and she wanted to have children.

Ravi agreed and said "तथास्तु" and put Akṣatā (अक्षता) on her forehead.

Then Ravi requested Neha to fulfill his wishes.

"यज्ञः मे कामः समृध्यताम्। धर्मः मे कामः समृध्यताम्। यशः मे कामः समृध्यताम्॥"

Ravi wanted her to support him as he worked hard to earn money, support the family and be successful by following the right way of living.

Neha agreed and said "तथास्तु" and put Akṣatā (अक्षता) on his forehead.

Ravi and Neha also read their personal and emotional vows to each other with a commitment to love and cherish each other for the rest of their lives.

Pāṇigrahaṇam (पाणिग्रहणं)

Ravi and Neha held each other's hands and said to each other.

"गृभ्णामि ते सौभगत्वाय हस्तम्, मया पत्या जरदष्टी: यथा असः।
भग: अर्यमा सविता पुरन्धि, मह्यम् त्वा दुर्गार्हपत्याय देवाः॥"

They repeated this verse in English as well.

"I take your hand in mine, which will bring me happiness,I ask you to live with me, forever, here and after, Various Gods have bestowed, your companionship upon me, That I may fulfill my Dharma, as a householder with you!"

Ring Exchange

In Hindu weddings, we do the ring exchange at the engagement ceremony. In the Indo-American weddings, we do it on both occasions. The wedding ring is a complete circle, the symbol of the cyclic nature of life and time. It is a symbol of auspiciousness, peace and unity, in which we join the couple's lives together.

Ravi and Neha exchanged the wedding rings with a clapping approval from all the guests.

"हिरण्यगर्भ सम्भुतम् सौवर्णम् च अन्गुलीयकम्! सर्वप्रदम् प्रयच्छामि प्रीणातु कमलापति:।।"
"I offer you the golden ring that Brahmā, the Creator produced. Let Vishnu be pleased with this offering."

Maṅgala Sūtra Bandhanam (मङ्गलसूत्र बन्धनम्)

Ravi did one of the most significant rituals of the whole ceremony - The Maṅgala Sūtra Bandhanam.

The Mangalsutra is a beaded necklace with two golden cups, one representing each family. By wearing this most important symbol for a married woman, the bride signifies strengthening the harmony between the two families.

Ravi tied the Maṅgala Sūtra, around Neha's neck to represent the strength of their mental union.During the Maṅgala Sūtra Bandhanam, Ravi said to Neha:

"सूत्रं मांगल्य संयुक्तं कण्ठे बध्नामि ते प्रिये।
सौभाग्य प्रीती सौहार्द ध्योतकं सुमनोहरम्।।"

"I am putting this beautiful Maṅgala Sūtra on you as a symbol of good luck, friendship, and our mental union."

The Maṅgala Sūtra Bandhanam is a mental union of the couple. It represents the sealing of their promise to fulfill each other's wishes by putting a marriage symbol) on each other's forehead, the seat of the mind and intellect. Ravi put an auspicious red Sindor (सिन्दूर) in her parted hair and Neha put a chandan tilak (चन्दन तिलक) on his forehead.

Vivāha Homa (विवाह होम)

The couple now takes the sacred pledge of marriage in the presence of the holy fire, Agni. This pledge, called Vivāha Homa, is the centerpiece of the Hindu Vedic Ceremony.

Agni assumes a great importance in all the Hindu Saṃskāra. He is the Gṛhapati-गृहपति, the lord of the house. He lights the domestic hearth in the kitchen, the main gathering place in every home. Without fire, there is no heat, there is no light, and indeed, there is no life! It is the symbol of family unity and social relations. The fire is a purifier and a sustainer of life. It also represents the internal fire that will keep the couple's marriage together.

Water is one of the most important items needed to start a new household. Kavita gave it to Neha at Kanyādāna. Fire is the other required item, which comes from the groom's father. Therefore, Ashok had the honor to light the fire for the Vivāha Homa to pass on the fire from his home to his son's new household.

The groom's first duty after marriage is to keep this fire burning at home, creating a happy and prosperous life and then pass it on to his son at his wedding ceremony. Hence, the groom offers ghee-the clarified butter- to the fire as the oblations to keep it burning, with the bride touching his right hand.

During the Vivāha Homa, Ravi and Neha requested various deities for a long and happy married life, using fire as the messenger. They also requested for abundant harvests, joys on earth, protection from adversaries, long life for their sons and daughters, elimination of sorrow and harmonious thinking among all.

Ravi was careful not to put too much ghee on the flames, as he was aware of the famous verse.

"घृतकुम्भसमा नारी तप्ताङ्गारसम: पुमान्।"

"A woman is like pot full of ghee and a man is like a hot burning coal." In the right amount, they work together very well; but too much of either may have adverse consequences!

After the guests gave their blessings by saying "तथास्तु", the couple entered the Gṛhastha Āśrama, the second stage of their lives.

5.3 The Spiritual Bond

Asha and Priti tied the knot, called Granthi Bandhanam, between Sneha's saree and Ravi's shawl. This is probably the most celebrated and the most photographed knot of the Hindu wedding ceremony.

The Vadhu-Vara-Vastra-Bandhanam (वधू वर वस्त्र बन्धनं) is the spiritual knot. representing the final two objectives, Dharma and Mokṣa, which are unique to human beings only. The married couple must follow Dharma in their married life whereas the pursuit of Mokṣa is an individual endeavor.

Lājāhoma (लाजाहोम:), Agni Pradakṣiṇa (अग्नि प्रदक्षिणा) & Aśmārohaṇam (अश्मारोहणं)

Neha, with Ravi holding her hands below hers, offered oblations to the holy fire with Lājā (लाह्या), popped corn, given to her by her brother, Neal. With each oblation to a different deity, Ravi prayed for a smooth transition for her to his home.

As they circled the Agni, he asked her to be his Sahadharmchārini (सहधर्मचारिणी) - a complementary and an equal partner in his pursuit of Artha, Kāma and Dharma.

"ॐ अमो अहं अस्मि, सा त्वम्। सा त्वं असि, अमो अहम् ।ध्यौरहम, पृथिवी त्वं। सामाहम्, ऋक् त्वम्।तावेव विवहावहै। प्रजां प्रजनयावहै। संप्रियो, रोचिष्णू, सुमनस्यमानौ, जीवेव शरद: शतम्॥"

"I am the Puruṣa (पुरुष); you are my Prakṛti (प्रकृति). I am the

sky; you are the earth. I am the song, you are the verse; I am the ocean, you are the shore. I am the strength but you are the beauty. We will live together lovingly and bring up our progeny. We will lead a joyful life of a hundred years".

Ravi then asked Neha to be strong and firm as the stone she ascended to face all the potential difficulties in their future married life.

"इमं अश्मानं आरोह, अश्मा इव त्वं स्थिरा भव।"

Neal would be Neha's pāṭhīrākhā (पाठीराखा)-a guardian, a person who would look after her future well-being. Earlier, it was Kishor, Neha's māmā, who brought Neha to her wedding. Now, Neal, as the future māmā, would escort Neha's future daughter to her wedding, 25-30 years from now. He twisted Ravi's ears hard to remind him to take good care of his sister.

Saptapadī (सप्तपदी)

Saptapadī, taking the seven vows, one with each step, is the legal step of the Hindu wedding ceremony. In the traditional ceremony, the groom states and asks the bride to follow those vows. With changing times, it is more appropriate they jointly say those vows to each other.

Ravi and Neha held their hands together and took seven steps from back to the front of the maṇḍapa. At each step, they promised each other to lead their married life with the following seven vows.

"1. इषे प्रथम पद-न्यास:।

Let us take the first step - to provide for and support each other.

2. ऊर्जे द्वितीय पद-न्यासः।

Let us take the second step - to develop mental,& spiritual strength.

3. रायस्पोषाय तृतीय पद-न्यासः।

Let us take the third step - to share our worldly possessions.

4. मायोभव्याय चतुर्थ पद-न्यासः।

Let us take the fourth step - to acquire knowledge, happiness and peace.

5. प्रजाभ्यः पञ्चम पद-न्यासः।

Let us take the fifth step - to raise strong and virtuous children.

6. ऋतुभ्यः षष्ठ पद-न्यासः।

Let us take the sixth step - to enjoy the fruits of all seasons.

7. सखा सप्तम पद-न्यासः।

Let us take the seventh step - to always remain friends, cherish, and respect each other. "

After they completed those vows, I brought their heads close together.

All the guests said "तथास्तु".

Saptarṣi-Dhruva Prārthanā (सप्तर्षि ध्रुव प्रार्थना)

Traditionally, the couple sees the Big Dipper and the North Star at night to pray for a very close and stable marriage.

The Big Dipper constellation is composed of seven bright stars, called the Saptarṣī, the seven sages, who are our ancestors. If you closely look at the middle star of the handle, you will actually see a binary star, a two star system, each revolving around the other. They are Sage Vaśiṣta (वशिष्ट) and his wife Arundhatī (अरुन्धती). Arundhatī is the epitome of chastity, conjugal bliss and wifely devotion. Just like that binary star, the couple should revolve around each other for the rest of their lives. If you draw a straight line from the last two stars of the ladle northwards, you see the North Star or Dhruv, the most stable star around which all stars seem to rotate from the Earth.

Ravi and Neha would look at the North Star and Big Dipper at night using the Skymap, but they prayed now for their marriage to be as stable as the North Star and as strong as that of Vaśiṣta and Arundhatī. In some regions, the Paṇḍita might have asked them to pray to the Sun during the daytime.

Āśirvāda (आशीर्वाद:)

Now, it was time for all family members, relatives and friends to welcome the newly married couple into the second stage of married life, the bedrock of any society with their own blessings for a happy married life. All repeated after me.

"ॐ ईहैव स्तं, मा वि यौष्टम्,
विश्वं आयु: वि अश्नुतम्॥
क्रीळन्तौ पुत्रै: नप्तृभि:,
मोदमानौ स्वे गृहे॥"

"May you fully support each other, in the journey of your lives. Let your lives be one, one soul residing in two bodies. May your lives be woven together, with a strong fabric of love, harmony and peace. Lead a full life of joy, with family, friends and children. May God bless you!

"ॐ तत सत्। ॐ तत सत्। ॐ तत सत्॥"

Formal Announcement

After the blessings, I announced Ravi and Neha as Husband and wife as the DJ played a very happy, celebratory song.

"Ladies and Gentlemen, It is my great pleasure to present to you, Mr. and Mrs. Ravi & Neha Mathur."

Recessional

After the couple took the blessings from their parents in the maṇḍapa and the elders in the first row, they walked down the aisle as the guests showered them with flower petals. They were followed by, bridesmaids and groomsmen, Asha and Priti and then by Kavita and Susan together and lastly by Ashok and Vijay together- a true union of the two families.

We completed the ceremony, right on schedule at 12:20 pm. Now, it was time for photo shoots with all the family and friends. However, Ravi had to pay a big bribe to get his shoes back from Priti and others as they kept them tossing back and forth.

Marriage Certificate

Soon after a delicious lunch, Julie brought the marriage certificate for me to sign. The Texas law states that the Christian Priests, Rabbis and the Judges can sign the certificates. Priests from other religions also can sign the certificate if the ceremony is conducted according their religion and the couple and congregation accepts the officiant with that authority. It was a pleasure to sign the certificate to induct this beautiful couple into Gṛhastha Āśrama.

5.4 Celebration

The evening reception is everybody's favorite part of any wedding. As I was enjoying the appetizers with a glass of cabernet, Kishor stopped by.

"We attend so many weddings in India; but this is the first time, I really understood the significance of the various rituals." Kishor said.

We chatted with a few more guests until it was time for the formal dinner. After the traditional processions of the bridesmaids, groomsmen, the siblings and the parents, Ravi and Neha entered the room for a standing ovation.

The evening program proceeded smoothly with Neal and

Asha again as the Masters of ceremony. There were traditional speeches as well as some entertainment. During the delicious vegetarian dinner, Vijay and Kavita as well as Ashok and Sushma stopped by each table to thank their guests and relatives for coming to the wedding and blessing the couple.

After dinner and some more socializing, we walked towards the elevator to go to our room when Asha and her colleague, Paul, stopped us in the hallway.

"Paṇḍitaji, now we understand the true meaning of tying-the-knot." Asha said.

"This is my first Hindu wedding. It was very logical, meaningful and deeply spiritual," Paul said.

"We are sure we will see you again!" Asha added.

6. PUTTING IT ALL TOGETHER

To plan and accomplish a successful Hindu wedding can be challenging, especially in a foreign environment. The India born parents, their American born children and the Paṇḍita may have altogether different ideas about the wedding events. I have tried to discuss and answer many of them with an example of a specific wedding. The hosts in this wedding followed all the correct "Do's "by evaluating pros and cons multiple options in each category. The results can be reviewed in the Appendix 7.1. If you can, avoid all the situations described in Appendix 7.2. I am putting it all together here with key takeaways as guide to a beautiful wedding.

Build A Triad Of The Couple, Parents And The Paṇḍita

The hosts should discuss with their paṇḍita what rituals, traditions, customs etc. they would like to follow, understand how he/she conducts the ceremony and mutually agree on the best ways to perform the wedding.

The couple should communicate with the parents and the paṇḍita their ideas about a fusion wedding and actively participate in understanding of the various rituals and their meanings. It helps a great deal if the couple provides the paṇḍita their background information to customize the ceremony as necessary

The ceremony and the associated saṃskāras are the most important among all the wedding events. They are one-third rituals, one-third explanations and one-third logistics. As such, the paṇḍita needs to fulfill multiple roles of a priest, a communicator and a manager. He or she can be an important advisor based on his years of experience in performing the ceremony. He can also suggest what works and what does not work in other events as well.

The Hindu weddings in western countries need to be better organized, relatively short, well explained, interesting and yet formal. The paṇḍit should o modify the rituals according to the couple's modern way of living and their concept of equal but complementary roles.

Even after all the discussions and communications, the couple, the parents as well as the paṇḍit benefit greatly from a rehearsal a day before. Do not skip it!

Resolve Differences

Many intergenerational, intercultural and interfaith issues can create significant difficulties in planning. They can spill over in the wedding itself if they are not addressed and resolved as soon as possible.

All issues should be resolved with compassion, compromise, logic, and love. The paṇḍita or some senior relatives, friends or a wedding planner can help you address these issues to make the events stress free and enjoyable.

Choose a Suitable Venue

Choosing a good venue is an absolute necessity for a beautiful wedding. The hosts' should choose a venue based on practicality, ambience, convenience and affordability. The paṇḍita can discuss the pros and cons of the venue and suggest if any improvements are needed. Based on my experience of conducting weddings in all sorts of venues, a single, local, suburban, four-five-star hotel works best for an elegant wedding. The hosts can manage various events effectively due to its multiple advantages such as accommodations, weather proof and controlled atmosphere with great ambiance, local vendors, 24/7 availability and many others.

The paṇḍita should pay special attention to the maṇḍapa design for a good flow, visibility, seat arrangement, and free area for the rituals.

Communicate and communicate well

Obviously, communication with the priest, with your guests and relatives, with all the vendors etc is a key part of a successful wedding. A well-designed, informative and current website is essential for all modern weddings. The website should include as much information about all the events, schedules, protocols, etc.

The Covid-19 pandemic has added more importance to timely information about the various protocols that all attendees need to observe. Your guests will appreciate a welcome letter with the latest schedule and information for all events.

Preserve Hindu Culture

Both parents should plan some of the Saṃskāras a few days before to discuss the Hindu way of life. Since the Vivāha Saṃskāra is the most important saṃskāra in anybody's life, it is an ideal set up to discuss the key tenets of the Sanātana Dharma. The paṇḍita should do them with full participation of family, relatives and friends. It takes a village to raise a child; it takes the whole society to strengthen the marriage, which in turn is the bedrock of any community.

Create a Minimum Stress Plan

Creating a project plan and taking into the consideration the smallest details is a key to the success of any wedding. Hiring a wedding planner can be helpful, especially if you have multiple events, a large guest list, a destination wedding and you are too busy otherwise!

Timing is an extremely critical element of the wedding events. Therefore, planning and management of schedules should be one of the highest priorities.

Provide a great Guest Experience

Indian hosts do a tremendous job in providing great hospitality to all their guests. Weddings are also a great social event. Therefore, to make it more enjoyable to guests, many of who come from far away and even for locals, the hosts should minimize unnecessary travel, avoid multiple venues, stick to the schedules and choose a comfortable hotel with amenities for good relaxation in between the events. A hospitality suite is always a nice place to meet and socialize.

Avoid the "Avoidable"

The appendix will give you examples of many situations that could have been avoided. It is a good idea to review all possible "what if" scenarios and plan accordingly right from the beginning. Expect the unexpected and plan for every possibility. It is a good idea to remember Murphy's Law - If things can go wrong, they will.

Go Local

Whether you choose your hometown venue or a destination venue, try to choose local vendors for all your needs; the paṇḍita, the maṇḍapa providers, photographers, caterers, sound-audio system technicians, entertainment groups etc. This will significantly reduce the logistics, expenses as well as travel complications.

Have Fun!

In spite of all the detailed planning, even after following all the guidelines in this book, something will go wrong! In the big picture, most of those will be minor details and only those in the wedding parry will notice them. It will all work out and the couple will get married. So, do not fret over some details that may not work out exactly the way you planned.

7. APPENDIX

This chapter includes feedback to the weddings and my own analysis of what did not work well in some weddings. I have also included information on some traditions, Muhūrta and the Ṝgveda wedding.

7.1 Perfect Weddings

Here is a sample of the feedback I have received from the couples and the parents who followed the approach described in this book. This will give you some idea that your clients are looking in a perfect wedding ceremony.

"Paul and I just wanted to send you a note to thank you

for doing such a wonderful job with our wedding ceremony. We cannot tell you how many of our friends and close family friends came up to us after the wedding to tell us how beautiful and spiritual the wedding ceremony was. You did an incredible job of explaining the steps of the ceremony to our guests (and to us!) and I know that everyone walked away feeling like they were truly a part of the ceremony. The wedding ceremony really touched so many people and we hope you know how much we appreciate that you came all the way to New Orleans to help us get married :)."

"Sheena and I have returned from our Honeymoon to the beautiful island of Fiji. I just wanted to send you a note thanking you for everything. We enjoyed the wedding ceremony the most out of all of the activities throughout our special weekend. Your work was just simply amazing! Everything ran on time and the audience was able to comprehend all of the important aspects of our wedding rituals. This meant so much to both Shital and I! Thank you again for conducting what we would like to say is the classiest Hindu ceremony we have witnessed to date"

"The wedding seems such a long time ago now, but the happiest memories from the day are still with us! Perhaps, it is a little selfish of us to think so, but we both sincerely felt that it was the best wedding we had ever been to! The ceremony you performed had so much depth, versatile enough for all to understand (including us!), but it maintained all the richness of our culture, religion, history and traditions. Most importantly, you reiterated all the values that we hold so dear to our hearts. We will always remember our vows to each other and our promises to the society (and we have the videos if we ever start to forget them!).

We thank you sincerely for performing a flawless ceremony for us!"

"We all express our heartfelt thanks to you for conducting Sheena's wedding ceremony. Everyone that I came across was full of praise for the way you conducted the rituals and without your permission, I took the liberty of giving your name to a few friends of mine who wanted to make use of your services. All the American friends of both Sheena and Michael were very pleased and gave us the impression that this was the only Indian wedding where they were able to understand very clearly, what was happening on the maṇḍapa because of your detailed rendition of the ceremony in English, which everyone present enjoyed."

"We would like to thank you for performing the Wedding Ceremony for our daughter. Wedding ceremony was great; we loved it and you performed very beautifully. We got so many compliments from our guests! They said it was the best wedding ceremony they have attended. Sir, Grahaśānti at our home was very impressive"

"We do not know how to thank you, as we were speechless of your performance at Shivani-Eshan's wedding. You made a history in our lives, as this was the most classy, elegant wedding for us. You have done a fantastic ceremony that each one who was there will remember this wedding forever. Thank you so much!"

"Ketan and I would like to thank you for conducting such a beautiful wedding ceremony for us. We received so much praise afterward for such an engaging, efficient and lovely ceremony. Our guests felt included and involved with what was going on. It was the most, also the quietest ceremony most have attended, and it was not too long or too short. Thank you for taking the time to meet with us beforehand as well and for being flexible with various things. We hope you enjoyed conducting the ceremony as much as we enjoyed being a part of it."

"The Grahaśānti Pūjā at home and marriage ceremony were the two most significant aspects of the wedding to all of us. Moreover, not only we felt so satisfied with how you performed those two pūjās, but many other attendees were very impressed too. All liked the fact that you stood and talked so clearly all through, you could get their attention and you conveyed the important points so well."

"Everyone had been raving about your performing the ceremony and told us that they thoroughly enjoyed the ceremony and the way you conducted it keeping everyone involved in it. Thanks ever so much for everything! Sarah's dad John mentioned to me that they and their friends enjoyed the ceremony especially the way you involve the audience in the ceremony."

"We want to express our sincere appreciation for the most beautiful wedding ceremony you conducted for our children. All the pūjās performed at various events were very informative and enjoyed by everyone. Our family members and friends have great compliments for you. Some of our young nieces and nephews ages 10 to 20 have already asked their parents to make sure to fly you to their hometowns for their wedding ceremonies."

"Once again, we wanted to convey our deepest and sincere thanks for the nice way in which you conducted the ceremony. It was very special and personal and everyone enjoyed it thoroughly.

Words cannot express our sincere thanks and gratitude for being part of our family and conducting the ceremony in such a warm, loving and caring way. Your great attention to details, professionalism and humor made it a very special occasion."

"Thank you for making Meena and Nate's ceremony very meaningful for them, our guests and us. You received many compliments on how well you conducted the ceremony and we were happy to have you join us for the festivities following the "pūjā ". We are grateful our paths crossed and we will not hesitate to recommend you to anyone who might require your services."

"We would like to thank you for the wonderfully orchestrated and very unique and special wedding ceremony you conducted for Neeta and Raj. Your rehearsal was necessary. You performed the wedding rituals in an hour and kept the audience captivated throughout! Many thanks for performing this for our children. It was a memorable wedding and we thank you for your blessings!"

"We wanted to convey our gratitude to you for conducting our amazing wedding ceremony in September. It was wonderful and all of our guests had such a great time and learned so much! The way that you explained the traditions was exceptional from your patience to your humor.

Thank you so much for coming to DC to perform our wedding. We deeply appreciate you taking the time to come a long way to celebrate our wedding with us. Our families enjoyed your company for all the events - cannot thank you enough for clearly articulating the significance of every step of the ceremony with the right amount of detail. It was everything and more than we had expected - felt like a fairy tale come true! For many of our guests, it was their first ever-Indian wedding experience and they thoroughly enjoyed every single second of the wedding ceremony."

"Thank you SO much for conducting such a lovely wedding for Ananya and Ashish. All the feedback I have received from friends and family is that this was a perfect event and probably the most beautiful wedding they have ever attended! They thought your officiating of the wedding was just wonderful and appreciated your clear but brief explanations, the spiritual meanings of the steps, the symbolism, the little bit of light humor, how you engaged the guests to bless the young couple, and the overall smooth flow of the ceremony. It really impressed everyone.

We also appreciate how much the rehearsal helped us in preparing for the actual wedding ceremony. Thank you so much for taking that time with us. It was very beneficial."

"Thank you for performing the most beautiful wedding ceremony for our children! It was truly elegant and magical! We appreciate the time you took to travel all the way to Cabo San Lucas and be away from your family. We will cherish the wedding ceremony memories forever!"

7.2 Preventable Situations

All couples, their parents, wedding planners and others work very hard to make their wedding memorable and enjoyable. Indeed all weddings do end up on a very happy note!

However, some events do not end up as expected in spite of all their good intentions, hard work and planning. The couple and parents are disappointed and wish they had planned for some of theses situations. In addition, the guests may also experience some discomforts like unnecessary travel, impact of some wedding delays on their own schedules etc.

I am listing some situations here so that the readers can take appropriate actions to learn from them.These situations have common threads of an outdoor wedding, lack of rehearsal, insufficient planning, unresolved conflicts and poor, infrequent communications.

We all know that one cannot predict good weather even a few days in advance, almost impossible to do so a year in advance. In spite of that, many couples plan their dream wedding in an outdoor setting. They will plan the minutest details about every other part of the wedding but leave it totally up to chance the main event!

Inclement Weather

Outdoor weddings can be spectacular but weather can be unpredictable. One cannot control the inclement weather itself but a well thought out indoor plan would have avoided many weather issues that required them to move the whole ceremony indoors at the last minute.

I was going to officiate a ceremony at a beautiful ski resort in Colorado. The couple had found a scenic spot at about 8000 ft elevation with a panoramic view of many 12-13000 ft mountains. The bride's parents and I took the gondola at 9:00 am to go to the venue where the wedding was supposed to be at 11 am. To our big surprise, there was hardly any activity at the planned site. The cell phones were not working at that altitude. After returning back, we found that the bride had changed the venue based on the inclement weather forecast at the time of the wedding. She had informed all the guests by a Face book post! Three hours later, we completed the ceremony at the hotel, indoor, where the weather was calm and comfortable.

At an outdoor wedding, a big dark cloud came out of nowhere. It started raining, just at the time the couple was garlanding each other. They had to move everything indoors but the inside facilities were too small to accommodate all the guests; so many guests were left standing throughout the ceremony.

Once, unbelievably, it was too cold in Houston! The venue had anticipated the cold weather; however, there were not enough heaters for the large number of guests. After moving indoors with significant delay, the host wanted to make sure that the maṇḍapa alignment was East-West; which caused further delays and not enough seats for all the guests.

Uncomfortable weather

In many instances, the weather was not so bad that they had to move the ceremony indoors. However, it was either uncomfortable for the guests or unsuitable for a good Hindu ceremony.

At three different weddings, we literally built a human wall so that we could keep the wind away to light the fire. At a beach wedding, it was so windy that I asked the couple to "imagine" that there was indeed a fire! They dutifully did their oblations to that imaginary fire. At still another wedding, a strong blast of wind knocked the canopy right over the fire.

At a wedding on a lakeshore, the wind was strong enough to topple all the stacks of decorated pitchers. They filled them with rocks to make them more stable; even then, four young men had to hold on to them throughout the ceremony.

In another instance, the organizers had expected it to be hot; so they had put portable air conditioners in the maṇḍapa. All of us in the maṇḍapa were comfortable, but the guests sought shelter under surrounding trees from the blazing Sun. Pretty soon, half the guests were missing from the audience. Yes, the Sun can be unbearable if you have to sit for an hour even in the relatively mild 75 F weather.

Great Outdoors, Poor Facilities

In general, outdoor venues are for small weddings with short ceremonies and few guests. They may have indoor halls, but they may be too small for Indian weddings. One should confirm that these are large enough to accommodate your planned guest list. If the facilities aren't large enough, then some guests may not be able to be accommodated in case of inclement weather.

I have seen 125 guests jammed in a 75-capacity reception hall. Can you imagine the anguish one has to go through to limit the guest list just because the venue can accommodate only so few people?

Some facilities have changing rooms only for the bride and groom's side. I have changed myself either in my car or in the restroom.

In general, the outdoor venues do not provide a stage or a platform on which we can set up a maṇḍapa. This creates poor visibility for a large audience. If the maṇḍapa is set on the ground, it can be difficult to do bare feet ceremony. It is also not proper to set up our deities in the open area for potentially adverse conditions.

I have also encountered a situation in an arboretum where they had dug up the area around the ceremony site for the spring planting. The hosts had selected the venue the summer before when all the flowers were in full bloom.

Outdoor facilities are also harder for women. Think hairdos, makeup, high heel shoes, saris, lack of close restrooms; you get the idea.

Limited Time Availability

Some venues may not be open every day and will commit only an hour for the rehearsal. As a result, I have ended up doing many rehearsals at the hosts' homes. Some venues have limited, say, an eight-hour slot for the ceremony, cocktails reception and dinner. This time crunch should be avoided.

Historic but Impractical Venues

One of the weddings was at a historic hotel where many Presidents and generals had stayed since 1850s. It had beautiful surroundings spread over acres of hills, rolling meadows and meandering streams. Unfortunately, the planners chose an outdoor site, which took about 10 minutes to walk to from the hotel. They did provide port-o-let near the ceremony site!

Another historic site was on the banks of the Hudson River in upstate New York. It was hard to get to and about 20 miles from the hotel where everybody had stayed. The wedding ceremony went ok; but it poured during the reception; fortunately, the huge tent protected us well.

Outdoor Distractions

As a young girl, Shweta had enjoyed going to a specific park. Therefore, she naturally chose that park for her wedding. As soon as we started the ceremony, the nearby airport traffic control, five miles south of the park, changed the takeoff for the flights in the South-North direction. We had unwelcome flyovers every few minutes, right over the maṇḍapa.

There was a helicopter hovering over a public garden during a ceremony in Philadelphia.

Thus, there can be many distractions for an outdoor ceremony. In addition, guests may pay less attention to the ceremony than to the surrounding scenery. You can have curious onlookers if the site is not private. Therefore, we lose any semblance of formality or serenity for any wedding.

Bridal Delays

In some outdoor venues, the maṇḍapa sites were much farther from the main building. In a few cases, the brides had stayed back in their rooms and were waiting for somebody to come and get them; which resulted in unnecessary delays.

A few ceremonies were delayed because the bride's makeup was not complete. Similarly, a few receptions were also late because of photo shoots and the bride's hairdo and makeup needed to be different between the ceremony and the reception that followed. Even a 2 hr cocktail hour was not enough; so all guests were kept waiting.

Some guests leave the receptions if the dinner is going to be very late.

Last Minute Program Changes

In spite of having an approved program and a rehearsal, there have been many last minute changes to the ceremony. These changes include but are not limited to distribution of a different program, requests for changes and additional rituals, unexpected singing by senior ladies, gift giving during the ceremony, coming to the mandap to bless the couple, unexpectedly throwing flowers at some steps etc.

Multiple Venues, Multiple Problems

In order to offer variety, many couples choose different events at different venues. In a huge metropolis like Houston, it is not easy to drive to different parts of the city, far away from your hotel.

In one case, a bus driving the guests to a remote location broke down just at the foothill. Some Indian women, in their best saris, started walking uphill, until the hosts made alternate arrangements. In another case, the driver got lost in the hill country! GPS did not work; some people, very dependent upon GPS, got lost at the Colorado wedding.

In another instance, after an evening reception, far away from our hotel, many guests wanted to return early but they scheduled the first return bus to depart at 11 pm. To make matters worse, that bus came late.

Either ensuring all events at the same place or other planned venues are close together will help reduce stress on the wedding day."

Missing Wedding items

I normally send the list of the required items for the ceremony few months before the big day. At one wedding, just two hours before the ceremony, it became obvious that they had not brought any items. My wife had to run to their home and gather whatever she could find and rush back to the venue; the bride's parents were very oblivious to the turmoil.

At another wedding, they had the list but the person in charge, having done her daughter's wedding in Chennai, brought the items that she thought needed for a Tamil wedding. They had also paid extra dollars for the excess and unnecessary baggage to fly to the destination wedding.

Now, I make sure that I address this item at the rehearsal.

Interfaith Issues

Some Christian parents did not participate in the Hindu ceremony; some refused to pray to Śrī. Gaṇeśa.

One Catholic Church would not or could not change their rehearsal and wedding times, creating scheduling difficulties for Hindu pre-wedding rituals, rehearsal and wedding ceremony.

Kiran and Kelley wanted to get married by both Christian

and Hindu ceremonies, preferably back to back at the same venue. Mary's church would not allow me to officiate the Hindu ceremony on their premises. Therefore, Kiran approached a Jewish community center. They had no problem with the Hindu ceremony but they would not allow a Christian ceremony. Therefore, we ended up doing the two ceremonies at two different locations.

Fortunately, these incidents do not create any issues and the Hindu wedding ceremony goes smoothly.

Indoor Distractions

It is very distracting when the guests socialize among themselves or play with their young children during the ceremony.

It is also disrespectful to serve and eat any food during any of the Hindu rituals. At one temple wedding, there were clear instructions not to serve food in the main hall. Guess what! They distributed Mango Lassi and some snacks right when I started the Vivāha Homa.

Intergenerational Conflicts

A young couple wanted an hour long, pragmatic ceremony but the groom's parents wanted every Telugu ritual done the traditional way. I tried to back off in favor of a South Indian paṇḍita but the couple would not let me. I conducted the first few steps the couple wanted, and then the other paṇḍita started the rituals the way the groom's parents wanted. The paṇḍita completed all the traditional rituals at 1:30 pm to an empty hall; the guests already had their lunch and were gone.

In another ceremony, the groom's father had initially agreed to the program. He asked me to make a few changes at the rehearsal. However, at the ceremony itself, he changed the seating arrangement and then proceeded to direct the ceremony himself the way he wanted it. I just stood by; after all, it was *his son's* wedding.

Nowadays, I insist on making sure that the couple and their parents are on the same page on all aspects of the wedding. It is also a Red Flag, if all my communication is primarily with the couple only with no parental involvement.

Reluctance for the Rehearsal

Many Indian parents as well as many Hindu priests do not see the need for a rehearsal since they think they know the ceremony well and know what to do. Rehearsals can help work out logistics and make sure your ceremony the next day will flow smoothly. While rehearsals are a new concept in Indian weddings, it really helps to get everyone comfortable about the ceremony.

Once I drove four hours to reach the venue at the appointed time for the rehearsal. However, there was nobody at the venue! When I called, the bride's father nonchalantly told me that they were too busy that day and would not be able to come.

They had also invited some special singing groups from India to play various songs at different steps of the ceremony. I had no clue that they were going to be part of the ceremony. They played a Bollywood song after I finished the Saṃskṛta Mantras at each step.

Even after a rehearsal, some unexpected things can happen.

In one ceremony, when I asked the couple to exchange the garlands, the bride put her garland on herself. Hearing a little laughter in the audience, the bride quickly corrected herself and put the garland on the groom.

At another ceremony, I had asked the bride's father to give her the garland after she enters the maṇḍapa. When I signaled him to do so, he himself tried to put the garland on the bride.

In Mahārāṣtrian and Gujarāti ceremonies, we hold an antarpata in front of the groom as the bride makes her entrance. In one case, the bride's escorts held the antarpata in front of the bride as she was walking in! Imagine the expression on the photographer's face, as he was all ready to capture her big arrival.

Long Distance Catering

Some hosts want to serve their favourite food, even though they have to cater it from far away caterers. At a wedding reception, the hosts decided to cater the food from a specialty restaurant, from a town about 100 miles away. The delivery driver got lost on the way. Not everybody had cell phones in those ancient times of the late nineties. The local friends put together a quick meal for about 150 guests in the small kitchen attached to the hall. Just when we were all ready to leave, the food delivery truck showed up!

However, the hosts showed great compassion to the caterer. Instead of getting upset, they offered her refreshments and comfort as she was crying because she felt so sorry for her very late arrival.

At another wedding in Austin, the hosts ordered food from a very famous Houston Restaurant, 160 miles away. It did not taste good at all; maybe it was not freshly prepared or might have been heated and reheated because the reception started very late.

Very Late Dinners and/or inappropriate Food

Many receptions dinners started very late, some as late as 10:30 pm! It may not be a big problem for the younger folks but may be too late for the older guests and those locals who would drive back to their homes.

In general, Indian cuisine has been popular in western countries, as long it is not too spicy and too hot. I have experienced many dishes too hot for an average American taste.

I can understand if the hosts want to add a non-vegetarian dish to the menu to be good hosts, especially in an interfaith wedding. However, at least on two occasions, they served beef, a no-no for Hindus, for reception dinner. It is possible that the host Hindu family was respecting the wishes of the groom's family. In general, the hosts should tactfully explain to the other side that serving beef is inappropriate at any Hindu function.

7.3 Wedding Traditions

शास्त्रात् रूढिः बलियसि: - Traditions are stronger than Scriptures!

There have been many additions or changes to the original marriage ceremony described in Gṛhya Sutras (गृह्यसूत्र), -books on domestic rituals. These eventually became a part of the main ceremony.

When is the couple actually married?

Traditionally, the Hindu ceremony is complete after all key rituals as described plus any regional variations. In Mahāraṣtra, the Maṅgalāṣṭaka with garland exchange is so important that it is the only ritual guests attend. In the South, Maṅgala Sūtra Bandhanam is the most important step. According to scriptures, the Vivāha Homa is the transition point after which the couple enters into married life. Saptapadī, taking the seven vows, is the legal step according to Indian law.

Sequence of Rituals

I have given a rationale for the specified sequence for the various rituals. However, it may be different in different provinces and the preference of the priest. For example, in some traditions, the "Maṅgala Sūtra Bandhanam" is the last step. If the hosts insist on a specific sequence, I follow that one.

How many rounds are in Agni Pradakṣiṇa?

In North India, couples go around the fire seven times whereas in Mahāraṣtra and Gujarāta, they go around only four times. Which one is correct?

As stated earlier, Lājāhoma, Agni Pradakṣiṇa, Aśmārohaṇam and Saptapadī are four distinct steps, each with a different objective and significance. It seems some priests combine them into one-step.

During the Laja homa, the Vedic ceremony describes three rounds around the fire for the three deities, Aryamna, Varuṇa and

Pūśaṇa and for children, prosperity and long life. The groom leads all the three rounds, clockwise, by holding the bride's right hand. The last offering to Prajāpati is without going around the fire.

In some customs, they do four rounds, presumably for Dharma, Artha, Kāma, and Mokṣa, even though the last one is not the main objective of the Gṛhastha Āśrama.

During the Agni Pradakṣiṇa, the groom describes to the bride their complementary relationship. He also asks her to be as strong as the stone she ascends during Aśmārohaṇam. He also requests the Agni for her smooth transition from her parents' home to his parent's home. Thus, he plays the leading role in the first three rounds per the Vedic ceremony.

There is no Vedic ritual for four rounds. However, over the years, there is a tradition of four rounds, the bride leading the last one. This tradition achieves three main objectives. First, it indicates their equal and complementary relationship. Secondly, after the fourth round, the bride naturally moves to the left side of the groom, closer to his heart. Finally, she sits next to the groom's parents, thus completing her transition from her parent's home to his parents' home.

Some say that the four rounds are associated with four stages of life. This may make practical sense as the man leads in the first two stages, slowly detaching himself from household duties in the third stage and handing over the family duties to his wife in the fourth stage.

Saptapadī literally means seven steps and not seven rounds. As explained earlier, at each step, the couple takes a vow, with holy fire as the witness about their future relationship to each other.

Therefore, it seems to me that the tradition of going around the holy fire seven times is a combination of Agni Pradakṣiṇa and Saptapadī. No scripture mentions this combination.

Washing Groom's feet

It used to be a tradition in India to wash and clean your

own feet before entering any home. When we worship God, it is also customary to invite Him into your own home and wash his feet. During the marriage ceremony, the groom, considered Viṣṇu in the wedding, comes to the venue from his own village. Hence, the bride's parents welcome him by washing his feet before entering the maṇḍapa. However, it is not necessary; just a welcome at the entrance is sufficient.

Akhand Saubhāgyavatī Bhava

In this Gujarātī tradition, a few women give the bride a word of advice regarding her future married life and give her their blessings. Then the bride's mother gives each of them a gift.

Kansāra Bhojana

In some ceremonies, the couple feed each other sweets symbolizing their first meal. At one wedding, when I called for this step, a few women came to the maṇḍapa with all the ingredients, sat on the floor and actually prepared the Kansars, -the traditional sweets.

Fun Traditions

In the past, most of the Indian marriages happened at a much earlier age. The bride and the groom did not know each other well, nor did their families. In order to create a bond between them as well as other family members and to create a little fun during the wedding, many games or customs were added some of which are described below.

Kāshī Yātrā

Before the start of the rituals, the priest advises the groom about his duties as a future Gṛhastha, a married householder responsible for the well-being for his family. After listening to them, he gets cold feet and decides that the marriage is not for him and leaves for Kāshī (Vārānashī) to become a monk. Some older persons give him all kinds of promises to which he relents. Then, all is good.

Finding the Ring

The siblings hide the wedding rings in a narrow necked pot

filled with rice or milk. The groom and the bride put their hands to find each other's ring. Whosoever finds the ring first is the winner.

Who sits first, Bride or the Groom?

After the fourth round, whosoever sits the first will be the dominant figure in the marriage. Pointing this out is a good idea to make the ceremony interesting.

Stealing Groom's shoes

The bride's younger sister, who hates the idea of the groom taking her sister, steals the groom shoes when he enters maṇḍapa. By stealing the shoes, she feels she can delay the departure of her sister but gives in after she gets a big bribe. However, sometimes, this can way go out of hand! In two weddings, a fight broke out among the groom's friends to steal his shoes.

Lifting the bride/groom during the garland Exchange

The bride's brothers lift and raise her high so that the groom is unable to garland her, thus creating a little mischief.

Kāna Pilī (twisting Groom's ear)

After Agni Pradakṣiṇa, as the bride leaves for her husband's home, her brother reminds the groom that he needs to take care of his sister by twisting his ear hard.

Pulling the Groom's Nose

In a Gujarātī ceremony, while receiving the groom and his party, the future mother-in-law suddenly pulls his nose. Although she might not say, "protect your reputation, it is important" but that is the message here.

Western Traditions

Kissing the bride' is not a part of the Hindu wedding. I have actually seen a paṇḍita asking the groom to do this! Some other traditions like cutting the cake, bride-father dance, groom-mother dance, etc are also creeping into Indian wedding receptions.

7.4 Muhūrta

Many people consider that auspicious periods or moments, called the Muhūrtas, are necessary for an activity like any religious event, wedding, entering a new home, travelling etc.

During the wedding ceremony, the most important step in the ceremony must occur at that moment or during that period. However, that step may be different for different traditions in India.

The Hindu Lunar Calendar, called Panchānga (पञ्चाङ्ग), lists the general and specific auspicious times. It has 12 months, each with thirty days, each day called a Tithi (तिथि). The wedding season in India occurs typically in March, April, May, June, November and December (Lunar months- चैत्र, वैशाख, ज्येष्ठ, मार्गशीर्ष, माघ, फाल्गुन). Further, Monday (सोमवार) Wednesday (बुधवार), Thursday (गुरुवार), and Friday (शुक्रवार) are considered auspicious weekdays.

Tithi (तिथि) is the time it takes for the longitudinal angle between the Moon and the Sun to increase by 12°. A Tithi begins at varying times of the day and varies in duration; from approximately 19 to 26 hours. Corrected for time difference, it starts and ends at the same time for all locations on earth. However, according to Indian calendar, a Tithi for a particular day is the *Tithi at the Sunrise* at that particular location.

Amāvásyā (अमावस्या), the lunar phase of the no moon is inauspicious as it signifies darkness.

There are also auspicious Nakṣatra, Yoga and Karana. By looking at the couples' horoscopes, the paṇḍita decides the auspicious moment for their wedding ceremony. Because of these various restrictions, the Vivāha Muhūrtas (विवाह मुहूर्त) are very limited in any given year for the specific couple.

A daytime muhūrta is the 15th duration of the day between Sunrise and Sunset. Thus, a 12-hour day between Sunrise at 6:00 am and Sunset at 6:00 pm has 15 muhūrtas of 48 minutes, each classified as auspicious or inauspicious.

I leave it to the parents and the couple to plan the ceremony around an auspicious time or not, depending upon their belief system.

One of my friends had planned his daughter's wedding on a Saturday morning. Two months after everything was set, the bride's aunt from Pune told my friend that that particular Saturday was an Amāvāsyā (अमावस्या) and hence inauspicious. I sensed a panic in his voice when he called, as many of his relatives would attend the wedding and he wanted to make sure that that particular Saturday was still ok for the ceremony.

Yes, it was Amāvāsyā in Pune but not in Dallas. In Pune, Amāvāsyā was over at 6:45 am, 45 minutes *after* the Sunrise. Therefore, the whole day was still Amāvāsyā. Amāvásyā in Dallas, adjusted for the time 10.5 hrs difference, was already over on Friday at 8:15 PM and Saturday was the next Tithī, Pratipadā. My friend and his wife were very happy, although they did not fully comprehend the logic.

At another wedding, few days before the ceremony, the parents were told that they were doing their daughter's wedding during the two weeks of Pitṛ Pakṣa (पितृ पक्ष), a two week period devoted to remembrances of our forefathers. Of course, it was too late to change all the plans. According to "शास्त्र असे सान्गते", nothing in the scriptures says that one should avoid these two weeks for any religious ceremony.

Rāhu Kāla (राहु काल) is also considered an inauspicious period; it occurs every day at different times. On Saturday, it is between 9:00 am to 12:00 Noon for about 1.5 hrs, depending upon the Sunrise at that location. Many people in the US want to have a morning wedding just at that time. What is the solution?

I typically offer Grahaśānti as a pragmatic solution if the families want to avoid any inauspicious periods for all the wedding events. One of the primary purposes of Grahaśānti is to pray to all the heavenly bodies, which drive whether any time period is auspicious or not. Another solution is not to start the ceremony until Rāhu Kāla is over. If that is not practical, then the couple should complete the most essential and the legal step of the Hindu wedding, the Saptapadi, only after Rāhu Kāla is over.

7.5 R̥̄gveda Wedding

The origin of Hindu Vedic marriage ceremony is in the marriage hymns of R̥̄gveda, composed ~1500 years BC. The verses may have poetic imaginations, cosmic significance, and multiple meanings. As a result, there does not seem to be a consensus on the identity of the bride and groom in this very descriptive ceremony!

Some articles describe that the feminine form of the Sun himself is the bride named Sūryā. The composers describe this marriage as an explanation of natural cosmic cycles, a strong bond between the Sun and the Moon and a poetic imagination of two very visible heavenly bodies. However, the Vedic literature is full of verses describing the Sun always in the masculine form. Further, the hymn states that the Sun-God Savitar bestowed his willing daughter Sūrya on her Lord.

The Aśvins (अश्विन) are two Vedic gods, divine twin equestrians, sons of Saranyu, who is wife of Surya in his form as Vivasvant. They symbolize the shining of sunrise and sunset, appearing in the sky before the dawn in a golden chariot. They are the doctors of gods. Some articles describe them as the grooms because they won the chariot race and Sūryā willingly climbed into their chariot. Some state that they defeated Soma (सोम) in the same chariot race and won the right to marry her. However, further reading clarifies that Ashvins were not the grooms but the groom's men and they came to bring Sūryā to her husband's home.

Further, if Aśvins are the Vivasvant's sons, then Sūryā and Aśvins are sister and half brothers. This also makes sense, as Usha, possibly another name for Sūryā, is their sister.

Soma (सोम) connotes the Moon or Chandra (चन्द्र) as well as a medicinal deity in Hindu mythology. Chandra married the 27 daughters of Daksha. No other literature mentions Soma as Sūryā's husband except the Ṝgveda hymn. It explicitly states that Soma wooed the maid Sūryā and he was her first husband.

So, one can logically conclude that Sūryā, the Sun's daughter, also may be known as Usha, and half sister of Aśvins, married Soma, the moon, in a marriage arranged by Savitar, the Sun God.

GLOSSARY

Agni (अग्नि) The Sacred Fire is the Lord of the home

Agnikuṇḍa (अग्निकुण्ड) A specified shape container for consecrated Fire

Ahiṃsā (अहिंसा) Non-Violence in everything we do

Akṣatā (अक्षता) Unbroken auspicious rice grains used for certain rituals

Akṣatāropaṇam (अक्षतारोपणं) Blessing with auspicious rice

Artha (अर्थ) The first objective of human life, Home, Wealth, Security,etc

Āśirvāda (आशीर्वाद) Blessings offered by the parents and guests

Aśmārohaṇam (अश्मारोहणं) Stepping on the Stone to be as strong as the stone

Āśrama (आश्रम) A hermitage, A stage of life

Aśvinīkumāra(अश्विनीकुमार) Divine Horse Headed Twins

Ātmā (आत्मा) The Soul, The Self in all living beings

Aukṣaṇa (औक्षण) Blessings for Long & Healthy life

Bandhanam (बन्धनम्) Tying, Binding, Bond

Bhārata (भारत) Alternate name of India, after the ancient king Bharata

Brahmā (ब्रह्मा) 1st of the Trinity of Gods -Creator of the world

Brāhma (ब्राह्म) Of Brahmā

Brahmacarya (ब्रह्मचर्य) Code of Conduct for Student Life

Brahmacarya Aśrama (ब्रह्मचर्य आश्रम) 1st Stage of Life - Student

Brahman (ब्रह्मन्) The Universal Reality and Ultimate Consciousness

Brāhmaṇa (ब्राह्मण) The ones who understand and worship Brahman

Darśana (दर्शन) Seeing and perceiving a deity

Dharma (धर्म) The Right Way of Living, which supports Natural Laws

Dhruva (ध्रुव) North Star worshipped for its stability

Ferā (फेरा) Circumambulation around the sacred Fire

Gāndharva (गान्धर्व) Of Gandharvas,who are the Celestial singers

Gaṇeśa (गणेश) A deity worshipped as Remover of Obstacles

Gâyatrî Mantra (गायत्री मन्त्र) The most auspicious mantra in Ṝgveda

Grahaśānti (ग्रहशान्ती) Prayers to nine Heavenly Bodies to remove difficulties

Granthi (ग्रन्थि) A knot, A tie

Gṛhapati (गृहपति) Lord of the Home

Gṛha Praveśa (गृह प्रवेश) Entering a new Home

Gṛhastha (गृहस्थ) A married Householder

Gṛhastha Āśrama (गृहस्थ आश्रम) 2nd Stage of Life- Householder

Jñāna (ज्ञान) Knowledge, Education

Jñānakāṇḍa (ज्ञानकाण्ड) Knowledge based philosophical ceremonies

Kāma (काम) Physical and Mental desires and pleasures

Kaṅkaṇa (कङ्कण) Bracelets typically worn by women

Kānkshiṇī (कान्क्षिणी) The one who wishes (good fortune)

Kanyā-Āgamana (कन्या आगमन) Arrival of the bride to the wedding ceremony

Kanyādāna (कन्यादान) "Giving Away the Bride"

Karma (कर्म) Work, Duty,Rituals

Karmakāṇḍa (कर्मकाण्ड) Rituals based sacraments

Lājāhoma (लाजाहोम:) Oblation of parched grains to the sacred fire

Lakṣmī (लक्ष्मी) Goddess of Wealth, Consort of Viṣṇu

Māmā (मामा) Maternal Uncle

Maṇḍapa (मण्डप) A four pillared Canopy erected for the wedding ceremony

Maṅgala (मङ्गल) Auspicious

Maṅgala Ferā (मङ्गल फेरा) Circumambulation around Fire

Maṅgala Sūtra (मङ्गलसूत्र) An auspicious necklace

Māṅgalya (माङ्गल्य) Auspiciousness

Mātṛka Pūjā (मातृका पूजा) Worship of Goddesses

Mokṣa (मोक्ष) Self Realization, Liberation, Most important goal of human life

Muhūrta (मुहूर्त) An Auspicious Time period

Mundāvali (मुण्डावली)A face ornament worn at wedding, thread ceremony

Nāndī Srāddha (नान्दी श्राद्ध) Remembrance of Forefathers

Nirīkṣaṇam (निरीक्षणम्) Keen Observation

Páñca mahābhūtā (पन्च महाभूता:) The Five Big Elements

Paṇḍita (पण्डित) Priest, Scholar, Learned Person

Pāṇigrahaṇam (पाणिग्रहणं) Holding each other's hands

Pradakṣiṇa (प्रदक्षिणा) Clockwise Circumambulation

Prārthanā (प्रार्थना) Prayers to deities

Pūjā (पूजा) Worship of a deity

Pūjana (पूजन) Act of the worship

Puṇyāhavācana (पुण्याहवाचन) Pronouncing a day to be auspicious

Purohitaḥ (पुरोहित) The family Priest

Puruṣārtha (पुरुषार्थ) A goal or objective of human Life

Rāhu Kāla (राहु काल) An inauspicious time period named after the demon Rāhu

Rāma (राम) Hero of the epic- Rāmāyaṇa

Ṛgveda (ऋग्वेद) The oldest Hindu scripture, the verses of Knowledge

Samāvartana (समावर्तन) Graduation ceremony from Student Life

Saṃgīta (संगीत) A Music and Dance welcome party

Saṃkalpaḥ (संकल्प) Resolution

Saṃsāra (संसार) The Cyclical Concept of human life and the World

Saṃskāra (संस्कार) Sacraments done by parents on their children

Saṃskṛta (संस्कृत) Root language of all Indian Languages

Saṃskṛti (संस्कृति) Cultural Heritage

Sanātana (सनातन) Eternal, neither beginning nor end

Sanyāsa Āśrama (सन्यास आश्रम) 4th Stage of Life for Spiritual pursuits

Saptapadī (सप्तपदी) Taking Seven Steps together, each step with a Vow

Saptarṣi (सप्तर्षि) Seven sages of ancient India, ancestors of Brahmin Gotras.

Sat-Cit-Ānanda (सत्-चित्-आनन्द) Pure Existence Consciousness Bliss,Brahman

Saubhāgya (सौभाग्य) Good Fortune

Sīmanta (सीमान्त) Village border

Sindhu (सिन्धु) River Indus

Sītā (सीता) Wife of Rāma

Śiva (शिव) 3rd of the Trinity of Gods - Dissolver of the world

Snātaka (स्नातक) Graduated Young man from the first stage, ready for wedding

Sūrya (सूर्य) The Sun

Sūryā (सूर्या) Daughter of the Sun God

Sūtra (सूत्र) Multi threaded auspicious cord or string

Svayaṃvara (स्वयंवर) Self Choice marriage

Tantu (तन्तु) Thread, String

Upanayana (उपनयन) Thread Ceremony for induction into studentship

Vadhu (वधू) Bride

Vāgdāna (वाग्दान) Giving a Word, a promise for future wedding

Vānaprastha Āśrama (वानप्रस्थ आश्रम) 3rd Stage Of Life- Retirement

Vara (वर) Groom

Vastra (वस्त्र) Cloth

Vidāi (विदाइ) Bridal Send off

Viṣṇu (विष्णु) 2nd of Trinity of Gods- Maintainer of the world

Vivāha (विवाह) Wedding

Vivāha Saṃskāra (विवाह संस्कार) The Wedding Ceremony

Vivāhahoma (विवाहहोम:) Fire Propitiation at the wedding

Yajña (यज्ञ) Fire Worship

REFERENCES

1. Vivāha Saṃskāra : विवाह संस्कार -Dr. Siddheshwar Shastri Chitrav,Bhāratiya Charitrakosh Mandal, Pune, India.

2. Wikipedia: Wikipedia has a vast number of topics related various Saṃskāras, including the wedding.

3. Vivāha Saṃskāra -विवाह संस्कार-Hindu Mandir Executives' Conference, North .America

4. शास्त्र असे सान्गते! Ved Vāni Prakāshana, Kolhapur, India

5. The Wonder That was India- A.L. Basham, Rupa & Co, New Delhi,

6. Drik Panchang: drikpanchang.com

7. स्वयंपुरोहित: Bāpata Shāstri, Rājesh Prakāshana, Pune, India

8. Various books by Jñāna Prabodhini (ज्ञान प्रबोधिनी), Pune, India

9. Multiple, published reports in various media

10. Interfaith Marriage -Dr. Dilip Amin, Mount Meru Publishing

11. Hindu Saṃskāras - Dr, Raj Pandey, Motilal Banrasidass, Varanasi

ABOUT THE AUTHOR

Padmakar Gangatirkar

Mr. Padmakar Gangatirkar, an engineer by profession, has been officiating Hindu Weddings in North America over 20 years. He has developed a unique style of officiating them with a well-balanced combination of traditional rituals and interesting delivery that connects to the couple, parents and the guests. He conducts them based on authentic scriptures with focus on their significance with detailed logistical considerations. In this book, he presents a how-to-guide for these ancient rituals in a modern way to the present demographics without sacrificing their main objectives, depth and spirituality.

A self taught Hindu Priest, he continues to find ways to give maximum enjoyment to all wedding attendees within the time constrains and within the bounds of the scriptures. He would love to hear from the readers their questions, comments and their own experiences regarding what worked well and what did not in the weddings they witnessed.

He can be contacted via e-mail: pamag43@gmail.com

Printed in Great Britain
by Amazon

84366519R00078